Unpacking the fashion industry

Unpacking the Fashion Industry is about the social relations behind the production of women's fashion clothes in the UK. Spotlighting a side of the industry that the consumer never sees, Annie Phizacklea gives a detailed account of the industry globally, but particularly the small firm sector of fashionwear production in the UK, based predominantly on ethnic entrepreneurship and labour.

The relations of power within the industry cannot, Phizacklea argues, be seen simply in class terms because they are divided along gender lines and at the same time are cross-cut by the impact of racism and ethnicity. Without an appreciation of the interaction of these relations, says Phizacklea, we cannot appreciate how the industry has developed the way it has, nor why it continues to flourish, often on the basis of very cheap and flexible labour.

Well-known for her work in the fields of racism, migration and female labour, Annie Phizacklea is co-author of *Labour and Racism* and *White Man's Country*, editor of *One Way Ticket: Migration and Female Labour* and co-editor of *Racism and Political Action in Britain*. She is Lecturer in Sociology at the University of Warwick.

Unpacking the fashion industry

Annie Phizacklea

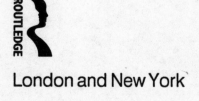

London and New York

First published 1990
by Routledge
11 New Fetter Lane, London EC4P 4EE

Simultaneously published in the USA and Canada
by Routledge
a division of Routledge, Chapman and Hall, Inc.
29 West 35th Street, New York, NY 10001

© 1990   Annie Phizacklea

Laserprinted by
NWL Editorial Services, Langport, Somerset, England

Printed and bound in Great Britain by
Biddles Ltd, Guildford and King's Lynn

British Library Cataloguing in Publication Data
Phizacklea, Annie
 Unpacking the fashion industry: gender, racism and class
 in production.
 1. Clothing industries. Personnel employment
 I. Title
 331.7687

Library of Congress Cataloging in Publication Data
Phizacklea, Annie.
 Unpacking the fashion industry / Annie Phizacklea.
 p.   cm.
 1. Clothing trade–Great Britain.   I. Title.
 TT504.6.G7P45   1990
 687'.0941–dc20   89–38993
                                                       CIP

ISBN   0–415–00054–8 (hbk)
       0–415–00055–6 (pbk)

Contents

Acknowledgements

This book represents the British component of a comparative study on the production of fashion clothing in Britain, France and the Federal Republic of Germany. The project was conceived in collaboration with my friend Mirjana Morokvasic of CNRS, Paris. We have published some of the collaborative material already with our colleague Hedwig Rudolf of the Technical University of Berlin.

The British component of the research was fully funded by the Economic and Social Research Council, to whom I am extremely grateful.

Introduction

Behind the pages of the glossy fashion magazines and catalogues, behind the seductive shop windows and interiors is a huge global industry – fashionwear. This book is about 'unpacking' that industry from the top, where those in control of the retailing end of the industry can expect to realise large profits, down to the manufacturing base, where they don't. For the vast majority of manufacturing workers in the industry – predominantly women – it means at best lower-than-average manufacturing wages and at worst, wages that barely meet the workers' daily, let alone long-term needs.

When we buy our clothes we give little thought to the people who make them. Sometimes we look at the label to see where the garment is made and it is likely that certain assumptions about the goods and their maker will spring to mind. These assumptions have become part of our 'world-view'. So for instance, if the label reads Taiwan, South Korea, China, or Thailand, it is associated with particular images. Images of low-paid workers sweating over a sewing machine for 12 hours a day making 'cheap' garments that will 'flood' or be 'dumped on' the UK fashionwear market, putting a British worker out of a job in the process. Like many such images it is only partly accurate and Chapter 3 attempts to unpack the concept of cheap import.

For a start it is not just clothing workers in developing countries who are paid very low wages for long hours. Homeworkers all over Britain can expect, in 1989, an hourly wage rate of around 80p with no job security or provision for periods of ill health, unemployment, or old age. In the pages that follow, evidence from a number of different sources is quoted that suggests that far from homeworking being regarded as an inefficient and uneconomic relic of the productive past, it is actually on the increase in the UK.

The second problem with our image of the 'cheap' import is who places the order for the garment in the first place? The answer is predominantly retailers in the advanced industrial countries, but also some 'manufacturers' who subcontract orders to low-wage countries.

The third problem with our 'conventional wisdom' about 'cheap' imports from countries such as China is that they are not necessarily cheap to buy. On a tour of the New Economic Zone in Southern China in early 1989, I talked with the director of a clothing firm based in the Midwest of the United States. He told me that his wife had paid $800 in the US for a US-designed dress made in China from Chinese silk. The workers in the New Economic Zone were earning £80–£100 a month. The economics of this situation was of course not lost on the director of the U.S. firm who concluded that it was economic madness for his own firm to go on producing standardised garments in the US where they paid their workers $8 an hour when they could shift production to Shenzen and pay a fraction of that in labour costs.

But it is argued in this book that the advantages of overseas production have not been as clear cut in Britain as they have for some of our European competitors, for example, the Federal Republic of Germany. It is suggested that in both countries, clothing manufacturers as well as retailers have sought and found cheaper labour through subcontracting production. Yet while manufacturers in the Federal Republic of Germany did this by subcontracting production abroad to low-wage countries, manufacturers in Britain have been more likely to off-load the unstandardised, short-run sectors of demand (fashionwear) and maintain flexibility by increased subcontracting domestically to the many small, inner-city firms dominated by ethnic entrepreneurs and labour. A major factor in explaining this difference is, it is argued, differing immigration policies. In the FRG, for instance, neither family migration nor self-employment has been encouraged, while in Britain it has largely been possible for the wives and dependants of male workers allowed in from the 'New Commonwealth' both to migrate and work without permits. The historical record indicates that access to 'family' labour is an important factor in establishing a small, labour-intensive business.

But the growth of such businesses in Britain could not have taken place if they had no role to play in the industry. Since the late 1970s retailers' increased demands for speed and flexibility on their suppliers have been met partially by these firms through the use of the subcontracting chain.

These small firms are run predominantly by ethnic-minority men who are located at the bottom of a 'dog-eat-dog' subcontracting chain. This chain means up to 200 per cent mark-ups even on British produced goods for some retailers, and paltry sums for the subcontractors, who survive at the expense of extremely low-paid workers and homeworkers.

All clothing workers are relatively poorly paid when compared to other manufacturing workers, but some earn only a pittance. Why is this? First, the clothing workforce is 80 per cent female, women being predominantly crowded into gender-specific, low-paid, and what is ranked as low-skilled work. As we shall see in Chapters 2 and 3, both historically and transnationally women's sewing skills learnt in childhood and adolescence are never adequately rewarded. This is because the acquisition of those skills is usually hidden in a sexual division of labour in the privatised sphere of the home where 'work' is unpaid and training rendered invisible. But Chapter 2 traces the way in which women's classification as low-skilled workers in the clothing industry is not just a result of the sexual division of labour within the family. The process has been reproduced and reinforced by the ability of male workers to define their work in the industry as 'skilled' and to demand a 'family wage'. In these circumstances, employers could pay women less because their work was not classified as skilled and they were not considered to be breadwinners for households. Male workers have hung onto those socially constructed skills, not just at the expense of women, but ultimately at the expense of their own jobs too. We shall see how in the high-productivity sector of the fashionwear industry this has meant that skilled tasks such as design and cutting, monopolised by men and commanding higher rates of pay, became the principal focus for the development and diffusion of deskilling and labour-displacing new technologies during the 1970s (the cost of this new equipment remains sufficiently high to keep it well beyond the reach of the myriad small subcontracting firms). Women may have replaced men in these 'new' jobs created by new technologies, but their work is regarded merely as semiskilled.

But there is a second, related reason why large numbers of clothing workers are paid so little. Many clothing producers have endeavoured to cheapen women's labour further by shifting production out of the factories altogether and into the workers' own homes.

The advantages for suppliers of production based on the labour of homeworkers are obvious for short unstandardised runs. As long as the work is completed on time by the homeworker, the supplier has only to cut the fabric and to make the delivery. The worker buys her own machine and pays all the remaining overheads and social costs of production.

But why are women prepared to work at home for 80p an hour? Primarily because they believe that homeworking will resolve their problems of child care (or the lack of it) set against their need to earn money. Britain is near the bottom of the league for under-fives' child-care provision in the European Community. As long as women are deemed primarily responsible for child care, mothers will be forced to find work that they can fit around child care. Unfortunately, homeworking rarely constitutes a solution with children requiring attention and their mothers constantly anxious about the child's health, safety, and quality of care. These are external constraints placed upon the employment options of most mothers of young children.

But black women experience further constraints in their employment options. Chapter 6 examines two of the ways in which racism and racial discrimination push black women into certain kinds of work. First, racism and sexism have been enshrined in immigration legislation institutionally relegating women to the position of chattels of men. The terms upon which many women have entered Britain as 'family' women have had a significant bearing on their subsequent integration into the labour market. Second, nationwide studies continue to demonstrate high levels of racial discrimination in employment. In addition, fear of racial abuse – or worse, attack – may mean that work in the relatively safe environment of the 'ethnic economy' or the home itself may offer an alternative employment structure for some minority women.

But the predominance of ethnic-minority men as small suppliers at the bottom end of the production subcontracting chain must also be seen within this context. As traditional job opportunities have shrunk – traditional in the sense that black men have been over represented in labour-intensive jobs in manufacturing since the 1950s – many ethnic-minority men have had little option but to pursue the entrepreneurship route. Their position is rarely that of the 'rags-to-Mercedes' immigrant, but more a transition from the lumpenproletariat to becoming a member of the lumpenbourgeoisie. But however subordinated a position these entrepreneurs occupy in the subcontracting chain, the position of minority women is even lower. In the course of fieldwork for this book no women entrepreneurs were encountered – they supplied the sewing skills that constitute the cornerstone of these small businesses.

What we are unpacking, therefore, is no simple capital–labour relationship. The 'capitals' in question are sometimes multinational, others are hand-to-mouth enterprises that compete for orders from the giant retailers, while at the same time being locked into a subcontracting stranglehold.

These capitalist relations of domination and subordination are in turn bound up with other sets of power relations that have their own dynamic. Women work *for* men, but rarely *with* men. But if these capital–labour relationships are gendered, they are also cross-cut by racism and ethnicity. Wave after wave of immigrant populations to Britain over a number of centuries have been excluded from mainstream opportunity structures and have carved out a niche in small labour-intensive enterprises, clothing manufacture being the most important. Ethnicity, or the recognition and maintenance of cultural difference, may in these circumstances cross-cut simple employer–employee relationships, but this needs to be understood within the context of racial exclusionary practices within white British society.

How gender, ethnicity, and class interact is not just the 'sub-plot' of this book. Without an appreciation of their interaction, we cannot fully understand how the industry has developed or why the sun refuses to go down on this so-called 'sunset' industry.

How fashion got unpacked

This research is part of a larger comparative study of fashionwear production in Britain, France, and the Federal Republic of Germany, paying particular attention to production in the traditional centres of fashion-clothing production in London, Paris, and Berlin. Some of the comparative work from this project has already been published (see Morokvasic *et al.*, 1986). The British research was fully funded by the Economic and Social Research Council and this book constitutes a full account of the British study.

A wide range of primary and secondary source material was used in compiling the information and at all stages I have used one source to check against another. The major secondary sources are aggregate statistical data published by the Business Statistics Office, particularly the sectoral *Business Monitor* series. Department of Trade and Industry statistics supplemented by the wealth of data contained in the *Hollings Apparel Industry Review* (formerly the *Hollings Statistical Bulletin*) were also important sources. Annual reports from the textile multinationals and larger manufacturers as well as annual Business Ratio reports constituted another valuable source.

Primary data collection was an additional source of information. In the first instance, key informants in the fashionwear industry were interviewed using the same checklist of questions regarding production, employment, and marketing trends within the industry. This included members of trade associations representing large, medium, and small firms. The latter supplied information for their respective associations and in some cases membership lists, which were an invaluable aid in the subsequent selection process of firms to be studied in greater detail. In addition, representatives of the National Union of Tailors and Garment Workers were interviewed at both national and local level. Interviews were also conducted with officials in the Clothing Economic Development Council and local government officials working in Economic Development Councils in Greater London, a number of London boroughs, and the West Midlands.

A questionnaire was sent to all the leading women's fashionwear retailers asking for information on their 'sourcing' policies (that is, where the garments that they sell are produced). Virtually all responded including C&A, who wrote to say that it was company policy *not* to reveal such information.

Primary data was also collected from firms and workers themselves. No claims to the representativeness of this sample are made, first, because it is a very small sample, second, because I concluded that none of the possible sampling frames was particularly reliable, and third, because I was more concerned that the interviews and on-site observations reflected the complete range of firms operating in London. Nevertheless, every attempt was made to screen out obvious biases. Thus at the *manufacturing level* twelve firms were randomly selected in London from a list compiled from two directories of women's fashionwear manufacturers. Five firms out of the twelve participated in the study by agreeing to both a factory visit and a personal interview with the proprietor or a senior manager. Three other manufacturers completed the questionnaire themselves and provided additional information either by mail or by telephone.

A rather different method was used for Cut-Make-and-Trim subcontractors. Directories in this case were supplemented by lists provided by both local government officials and trade associations. Again a random sample of twenty firms in East and Northeast London was drawn and in the first instance telephone contact was made with the firm. Two of the firms contacted in this way had moved from subcontractor status to manufacturer status. In other words, they had moved up the subcontracting chain while at the same time virtually moving out of production altogether themselves. They had become middlemen between retailers and subcontractors. These two firms were included in the 'manufacturers' sample.

Eight Cut-Make-and-Trim or Make-and-Trim subcontractors were visited and the proprietor interviewed (all of whom were ethnic minority entrepreneurs).

Thus the sample of London firms includes ten manufacturers of varying size and, as we shall see, supplying rather different markets. Some of these manufacturers maintain a purely skeleton staff. It also includes eight Cut-Make-and-Trim or Make-and-Trim firms. Thus every effort was made to cover the main range of types of firm in London in early 1985. No claims of representativeness are made for this sample but nor do I believe that the actual London firms in the sample are unusual in any particular way. If a firm seemed to be reluctant at first to participate in the study, I would usually simply turn up at the premises and in a number of cases this method resulted in an interview and time for observational research.

Access to workforces was more difficult. In only two of the London firms was access to the workforce obtained and the resultant interviews were not particularly successful as their replies were very guarded. Thus another method of interviewing workers was devised using two Bangladeshi community workers and a Cypriot who interviewed 17 workers outside of working hours and in their own homes. Again no claims of representativeness are made of the sample in so far as the respondents were all known to the interviewers through community work, relatives, or friends. The information gained from these interviews was shown to local trade unionists who confirmed that the variability in pay and conditions amongst the workers interviewed was in line with prevailing pay rates and conditions in the London clothing industry as a whole.

Outside of London, sampling was not random. It was deemed important to obtain information from what were regarded by the key informants as 'innovators' in terms of investment in new technology as well as firms that were continuing to use traditional methods of production. Two firms of each type supplied information for the study and this is used principally in Chapter 4, which addresses the impact of new technology in the industry. I was heavily reliant upon the key informants and other trade sources in estimating the extent of diffusion of new technology in the British fashionwear industry as a whole (though the findings of another study carried out at the same time by Cynthia Cockburn are cited in Chapter 4 as well).

Finally, three homeworkers in Birmingham and one in London were interviewed and the production chain followed back from them. At all stages of collecting information and evidence for the book, I have endeavoured to check one source against another.

Chapter one

Dress sense

Making fashion clothes in Britain today

Throughout the 1970s the British clothing industry became increasingly uncompetitive internationally, but it was in the space of four years that it appeared to have become a sunset industry. For instance, between 1979 and 1983:

1. production in the UK clothing industry fell by 29 per cent;
2. one third of the registered workforce lost their jobs (at the end of 1978 there were 307,000 persons registered as working in the clothing industry; in 1983 there were 207,400);
3. a crude trade deficit of £250.7m in 1978 had widened to £736m by 1983 (*British Business,* 1984: 598–600); and
4. imports were increasing three times as fast as domestic production in an industry where the rate of profitability is in any case much lower than in other sectors of manufacturing in the UK (Hollings, 1985).

In a labour-intensive industry based on a globally available technology, decline was blamed (somewhat incorrectly) on cheap imports and despite an increasingly protectionist stance against low-wage developing countries, producers in the developed countries were advised to 'automate, relocate, or evaporate'.

Within this overall picture of decline there are two sectors of the UK industry officially known as 'Workwear'* and 'Women's and girls' light outerwear, lingerie, and infants' wear' respectively, which appear to be more resistant to the inroads of what is termed 'import penetration' (which means the percentage of apparent home

---

* The 'workwear' heading includes men's and boys' jeans where import penetration is over 50 per cent. This is off-set within the heading as a whole by the very low level of imports amongst garments such as overalls and other protective workwear.

demand met by imported garments, see Table 1.1). The sector called 'Women's and girls' light outerwear' – more commonly known as the 'fashion trade' – constitutes the subject matter of this book. Worth £2.3 billion in sales to retailers in 1986, women's fashionwear has been the most profitable sector of clothing retail since 1980 and most of the orders from retailers in this sector continue to be supplied by British producers.

A major argument of this book is that the survival of fashionwear production in Britain in the 1980s would not have been possible on

Table 1.1 Output, import penetration and employment by sector of the clothing industry (UK), 1979–87

Output (1980=100); Import Penetration (%); Employment (000's)										
Activity O/I/E*		1979	1980	1981	1982	1983	1984	1985	1986	1987
4531	Output	110.5	100.0	83.5	88.7	91.9	92.9	103.7	115.5	112.6
	Imports	32.5	32.0	41.3	39.9	33.5	39.0	34.4	35.0	43.2
	Employ	15.2	13.3	11.9	11.8	12.6	–	–	–	–
4532	Output	122.9	100.0	88.8	85.9	88.1	93.2	100.6	103.3	110.9
	Imports	27.3	27.5	31.6	36.3	40.2	42.0	42.0	42.3	44.1
	Employ	58.8	42.3	35.6	33.5	35.8	17.5	–	–	–
4533	Output	112.7	100.0	90.0	93.1	89.3	89.6	94.5	94.3	93.4
	Imports	23.9	24.1	29.3	29.5	33.6	38.6	39.6	42.2	47.6
	Employ	35.6	28.3	26.0	25.7	22.2	24.9	–	–	–
4534	Output	106.6	100.0	88.5	89.0	104.5	120.3	118.0	128.6	126.1
	Imports	–	–	–	–	32.9	27.7	25.8	24.3	26.4
	Employ	–	–	–	–	–	16.7	–	–	–
4535	Output	105.0	100.0	92.2	104.4	106.2	106.9	135.4	136.4	134.9
	Imports	32.8	35.7	37.2	35.7	31.4	38.0	31.5	32.1	34.5
	Employ	39.1	34.1	31.4	31.7	34.9	–	12.3	–	–
4536	Output	108.0	100.0	94.3	97.6	99.8	100.7	115.9	115.2	111.7
	Imports	19.0	18.8	23.0	22.6	21.5	23.2	23.8	24.6	28.6
	Employ	93.9	81.5	76.9	74.4	77.9	89.5	–	–	–

Source: Output and employment figures are taken from the respective *Business Monitor* series and import penetration figures from the DTI, Bulletin of Textile and Clothing Statistics.

* indicates Output/Import/Employment

4531 – Weatherproof outerwear
4532 – Men's and boys' tailored outerwear
4533 – Women's and girls' tailored outerwear
4534 – Work clothes, overalls, etc.
4535 – Men's and boys' shirts, underwear, etc.
4536 – Women's and girls' light outerwear, lingerie, and infants' wear.
There may be some lack of fit between 1981 and 1982 figures as the most recent tables only cover the sectoral figures from 1982.

Due to no minimum Wage

such a scale without the presence of ethnic-minority entrepreneurs and labour as producers in this sector. The constraints placed upon employment opportunity structures by racism for minority men, and the additional constraint of gender segregation in labour markets for minority women, have played into the hands of a government whose aim has been to lower wages in large sectors of British industry. The result is a highly flexible sector of inner-city firms producing fashion-wear at prices competitive with so-called Third World countries and without any of the time and transportation constraints that overseas production carries with it. Flexibility in these firms is heavily dependent upon the casualisation of labour, particularly an increased use of homeworkers.

Retailers can now minimise risk and uncertainty by combining the benefits of improved information technology with access to fast and flexible domestic production sources. This is achieved through precise consumer targeting, more efficient 'just-in-time' ordering decisions, and rapid turnaround in the production of short runs and varied styles.

There have also been micro-electronically related innovations in manufacturing equipment, which unlike their dedicated predecessors are suited to short runs and frequent changes in style. Nevertheless, such equipment remains relatively expensive and well beyond the financial reach of the small-firm sector. In addition, the incentive to invest in such labour-saving equipment is greatly reduced if there is continuing access to cheap and flexible labour in Britain. In these circumstances the introduction and diffusion of such equipment is viewed as an expensive alternative strategy embarked upon by a minority.

Changing markets

The amount people are prepared to spend on clothing is elastic and as recession deepened by the end of the 1970s, consumption of clothing stagnated. This precipitated what came to be known as the retail battle of the 'high street giants'. As we shall see, British manufacturers ultimately paid the price for high street price-cutting wars and some large, but in particular medium-sized firms went out of business (Rainnie, 1984; Totterdill, 1988). In the meantime retailers began to research new strategies for revitalising the home fashionwear market. While demand had become increasingly unpredictable in mass-market terms, more money was spent in researching the market and targeting specific age and income brackets.

The under-25, high-fashion, low-price market is of considerable importance, but it is those retailers who have carefully researched and then targeted the over-25-year-old womenswear market who have made real inroads into the sector in the 1980s, in line with other aspects of 'lifestyle' retailing. Thus, what we are witnessing is a highly segmented market demanding even shorter runs and rapid changes in production than has ever before been the case. The old-fashioned cash register has been replaced in the larger chains by electronic point-of-sale equipment (EPOS), which allows retailers to analyse purchasing trends rapidly and precisely (e.g. styles, sizes, etc.). These are the data upon which new orders are based, orders that retailers want produced rapidly in line with demand. If one adds to this list increased sensitivity to demand, factors such as high interest rates, increased transport and insurance costs for overseas goods, reluctance to order forward and hold stocks, and a tighter control on quality then the attraction of having garments made in Britain rather than Hong Kong or Taiwan is clear.

Thus, high street price-cutting, high interest rates, and a new non-interventionist Government drove many larger clothing firms to the wall in the late 1970s and early 1980s. But many of the remaining established firms have also been bypassed by retailers in their search for the 'fully flexible' firm that could meet their stringent production demands in terms of time and quantity, in both cases, ever shorter. It is the growth of this small-firm sector that has thrived on the basis of these new demands and the class, gender, and ethnic relations that support its viability that are a major concern of the latter part of this book. As it is the sourcing policies of the big retailers that largely determine the fate of whole national industries, the strategies of women's fashionwear retailers and how they affect clothing producers are considered first.

What goes on behind the label?

Most women buy their clothes from shops, certain supermarkets, or by mail order – though the jumble sale remains both a favourite and a necessity for many who are not sharing in the benefits of the new 'enterprise culture'. Virtually all retailers have pulled out of manufacturing, preferring to let the latter shoulder the risks involved. A few retailers at the top end of the womenswear market, for example, Alexon, continue to manufacture most of their own clothes and other manufacturers with their own brand name often opt for the 'shop-within-a-shop' form of retailing. Nevertheless, the bulk of clothes that we buy will have come through a chain of subcontracted orders.

People from the post-war baby bulge who started buying clothes in the 1960s and who then constituted a youthful target group have of course grown up. And while there are still plenty of adolescents around to keep the kind of youth market catered for by Chelsea Girl profitably operational, it is women in the 25–44 year-old age group who now constitute a mass, but highly segmented target group wooed by elegant shop interiors and glossy 'lifestyle' mail order catalogues. The clothes on offer are undoubtedly more stylish, very often part of a co-ordinated range, and will probably be part of a much shorter production run than has ever been the case in the post-war period.

Unlike France and Italy where retailing remains highly fragmented, Britain in the post-war period has witnessed a rapid concentration of distribution amongst multiple-chain and variety stores who control 70 per cent of Britain's retailing in clothing. Their highly centralised buying power exerted a controlling influence on how British clothing manufacturing developed in these years. The average British woman spent less on clothes than her French, Italian, or German counterpart so a premium was placed on price rather than design in manufacture. As a result, profitable garment manufacturing centred around achieving economies of scale through long runs and the introduction of Taylorised (see p. 58) production methods.

But recession and changes in demography and taste forced a rethink in women's retailing patterns. It is estimated that at least 60 per cent of women's retailers revamped their image in the five years up to 1987 and even the most traditional of mail order catalogues have recognised that there is a market for designer clothes at reasonable prices (*Observer*, 15 May 1988). Up until 1983 the growth in consumer expenditure generally outstripped the growth in women's spending on clothes. But since that date the reverse has been the case.

Multiple-chain retailers such as Next and Burtons have acted as trendsetters in this retailing revolution. Both had their origins in menswear manufacturing and retailing and as this sector of clothing became less profitable, they began to move out of manufacturing (in the case of Burton's altogether) and into the more profitable retail sector and women's fashionwear. Next, which emerged out of the Hepworths men's tailoring stable in 1981, has developed a highly successful (in terms of profitability) strategy of luring consumers away from the more 'safe', relatively cheap, mass-marketed clothes to a new co-ordinated look that combines high fashion with good quality, but at prices well within the reach of the average working woman. By 1983 it was clear that the strategy had created a real demand in the over-25 year-old womenswear market (much younger women were also buying clothes at Next). In addition, Burton's, which was already targeting specific markets with its different chains (for example, the 15–25 year-old market with Dorothy Perkins), launched Principles in direct competition with Next. The trend away from racks and racks of similar dresses, shirts, etc., meant that retailing giants such as Marks and Spencer had to rethink their image if they were to retain their market share (*Guardian*, 24 October 1984).

In 1986, Next acquired Grattan, the mail order company, and launched the highly innovatory Next Directory in early 1988. This new mail order business claims a 48-hour delivery service from its automated warehouse.

Many of the changes that have occurred in women's fashionwear retailing would have been impossible without the introduction of new technology, such as EPOS. With the emphasis on short runs, retailers therefore minimise the risk of reaching the end of a season with dozens of lines that didn't sell. The company that has perfected this strategy is the much imitated Italian firm, Benetton.

The Benetton model

Fiorenza Belussi argues in her detailed study of Benetton that its novelty lies in an information system that links up a network of wholesalers and retailers with a large constellation of producers. In other words, she argues 'this model works as a combined strategy of 'just-in-time' systems in production and distribution' (Belussi, 1987: 4). Benetton represents an innovatory form of retailing in so far as the majority of its outlets are not owned by the firm but are similar to franchises except the licensees do not pay a royalty. Nevertheless, the full cost of setting up the shop is borne by the operator and they must adhere rigidly to Benetton interior design, shop organisation, and sell only Benetton brand names. In 1987 the turnover in Benetton shops amounted to £670m with a net profit of £48m ('From rags to riches' *Observer*, 22 May 1988: 56).

The organisational and labour costs of Benetton shops are much lower than comparable clothing shops in Europe or the US. There is no backroom stock-holding and everything is visible on the shelves of its 4,500 outlets worldwide. Benetton only produces goods in response to direct orders and both the pattern of sales and reorders are continuously fed back to the Ponzano headquarters by a private and exclusive information-technology network. Belussi argues that it is this information network, supported by a particular organisation of production, that both reduces costs and makes Benetton highly responsive to market trends while minimising uncertainties and risks. The strategy allows the firm to reach the market 6–8 weeks in advance of its competitors and to respond to reorders within 10 days (Belussi, 1987: 49).

What is of very real interest is that the production system itself mixes state-of-the-art technology with the most traditional forms of production including homeworking. Set against the rapid expansion of Benetton outlets and sales worldwide (remember Benetton does not directly employ people in its shops, the licensee does), there has been a very low increase in Benetton employment. This is explained by the fact that Benetton subcontracts all the labour-intensive stages of its production. 'Internal' production is restricted to design, size grading, and cutting and at the end of the production cycle, dyeing, quality control, packaging, labelling, warehousing, and delivering. In short, all the processes that are capital-intensive.

For knitwear alone there are around 300 firms concentrated in the Treviso area employing 15,000–20,000 workers (Belussi, 1987: 31). Typical firm size is small, 20–40 employees, and Belussi argues that 'the growth of the new firms is focused on the centrality of the family's members' (ibid.: 9). The development of Benetton follows a pattern characteristic of this region in Italy. It is a pattern of new industrial growth led by entrepreneurs drawn disproportionately from skilled manual backgrounds. Luciana and Guiliana Benetton both worked from an early age in the knitwear and textile industry and in the late 1950s they branched out on their own. Luciana would get orders for knitwear and Guiliana would make them up. Essentially it is a division of labour (now marketing and design) that continues to characterise their roles within the family firm.

While Benetton subcontracts all the least-skilled sectors of production to small local firms, it maintains total control of the production process overall. In addition, it gives advice on management, equipment, and work organisation to its subcontractors. The two main advantages of the subcontracting system are, Belussi argues, the use of external managerial resources and a significant reduction in labour costs, around 40 per cent (ibid.: 28).

What we are witnessing, therefore, in Benetton's highly successful strategy is what I would term 'the best of both worlds'; reaping the benefits of new technology and the cheaper labour costs of the subcontracting system, while minimising risk and uncertainty. It is, as we shall see, a strategy that is being pursued increasingly in Britain and goes a long way to explaining the relative vitality of women's fashion-wear production.

Retailers and producers: an uneven game

The relationship between retailers and clothing producers does, of course, take a number of forms, with many retailers preferring to maintain an arm's-length relationship with the producer, their only concern being that the goods arrive on time and at the right price and specification.

Eileen Davenport unpacks this arm's-length relationship as it applies to C&A and its suppliers (50 per cent of whom were overseas in 1985):

> The net effect of this arm's length strategy has been to perpetuate and encourage a vast subcontracting network. Once C&A places an order with a manufacturer, it is then the responsibility of the manufacturer to produce the order at the right price, to an agreed quality standard and to meet the deadline. The order itself may be subcontracted through more than a dozen firms. For the larger firms in the chain and the retailer, the process of subcontracting can be lucrative. Coats selling for £69 in C&A in November 1983, for example, started out as 'coat shells' manufactured by a small unit in Spitalfields, East London. The manufacturer received £2.50 for each coat shell from the next firm up the chain. Of this £2.50, 25p appeared as profit for the manufacturer; for the ten Bengali

How much mark up

workers wages were correspondingly low.

(Davenport, 1988, quoted in Totterdill, 1988: 7)

Nevertheless, there is evidence to suggest that this relationship is changing with some retailers at least. Undoubtedly some clothing retailers have begun to develop their ranges in close collaboration with manufacturers (Zeitlin and Totterdill, 1988: 9). But developing a closer relationship with a retailer or retailers may not be as cosy a solution as it sounds, nor a solution to the problems of declining profitability that British clothing producers have and continue to face. For instance, Marks and Spencer, which sources 90 per cent of its garments in the UK (many people in the industry whom I interviewed for this book believed that there would not be a British clothing industry without M & S), has always maintained a close relationship with its suppliers but in periods of reduced profitability, which is a euphemistic way of describing what happened between 1979 and 1983 in Britain, the relationship may be far from cosy.

Al Rainnie's analysis of the Marks and Spencer/manufacturer relationship illustrates both sides of the coin. First a view from *Management Today*, November 1980:

> Traditionally M & S has played benevolent dictator to its
> suppliers, giving them exact specifications for an acceptable
> item – the number of stitches to an inch, the number of inches
> in a hem – and rewarding them with huge orders that allow long
> production runs.

> (quoted in Rainnie, 1984: 150)

But that reward can be bought at a high price in employment terms. Angela Coyle's highly original account of women clothing workers' experience of redundancy and unemployment due to the closure of two factories in Yorkshire in 1980 makes salutary reading. Interviewing the former manager of one of the factories in Castleford, she explained the closure as follows:

> It was more efficient, however you measure efficiency.... But at
> that time Carrington Viyella (the parent company) were
> desperately trying to get into the Marks and Spencer market in
> trousers. We do a lot with M & S, but nothing in trousers. We
> had made them at Castleford for M & S, but M & S didn't like
> the Castleford factory because it was small and a bit grubby and
> the ladies' toilets weren't really up to M & S standards, the

> canteen wasn't very clean and they didn't like the cook ... that
> sort of thing. Castleford just wasn't an M & S type of factory,
> but this (Tadcaster) is.... Also at that time capacity came into it.
>
> (Coyle, 1984: 25)

In their 1979 review of the clothing industry the *Investors Chronicle* argued that: 'even where UK manufacturers are managing to hold their share of the market, they are often doing so at the cost of reduced margins – because of tight cost controls by retailers, notably Marks and Spencer' (quoted in Rainnie, 1984: 150); and the *Sunday Times* on 28 February 1982 had this to say about the relationship:

> Always a hard taskmaster, M & S is being increasingly choosy
> and in the last few months has axed several of its suppliers,
> forcing some to close. . . . The losers are the small companies,
> some of them part of larger groups, but mostly independents,
> particularly clothing manufacturers, which are regularly
> collapsing into the statistics of company failures.
>
> (quoted in Rainnie, 1984: 50)

In 1979, M & S chose to join the battle of the high street giants by moving away from the medium to high priced market and into the medium to low priced bands. It expected its suppliers to shoulder half of the price cuts (ibid.: 151). Obviously, Marks and Spencer was not the only retailer who attempted to pass on some of the squeeze in profits onto its suppliers. In his *Inside the Inner City*, Paul Harrison quotes from one Hackney manufacturer in 1979, who perhaps in his first sentence sums up precisely the unpredictable nature of the retailer–producer relationship: 'Whatever you've done in the past counts for nothing – you can't save up goodwill in a competitive tender. People are looking at price, price, price, all the time. I've had to reduce my prices lower than 1978 to compete' (Harrison, 1983: 54). For those producers who survived the high street price-cutting war of 1979, it was this year's goods at last year's prices. For others it was sudden death, particularly for those producers who had dealt solely with one client. 'One day the client walked in and informed the manufacturer that henceforth he would be placing his orders in Paraguay' (ibid.: 53). Or if the firm was a cog in one of the textile-conglomerates apparatus, all of whom underwent massive reorganisation, restructuring, and rationalisation during the same period with certain plants simply not figuring in the corporate strategy for survival, then the result was the same (Coyle, 1984: 21).

But the three leading textile conglomerates (Courtaulds, Tootals, and Coats Viyella) control a far smaller share of sales in women's fashionwear (16 per cent) than in other areas of clothing. For instance, in men's shirts they control nearly 40 per cent of sales (not all of which are manufactured in the UK) and in underwear, 50 per cent (*Business Monitor, PQ1006*, Business Statistics Office, various dates).

Women's fashionwear remains the domain of the small independent producer with 72 per cent of all units in the sector employing less than 10 people (*Business Monitor, PA1003*, Business Statistics Office, 1987). The advantages for retailers of a sector dominated by a huge number of small firms are clear. Rainnie suggests that the large retailers gain a great deal in reduced production costs by having a large number of suppliers who will compete with each other for their favours (Rainnie, 1984: 154). But the competitiveness and unpredictability for the suppliers militate against their investing in productivity-enhancing and therefore labour-saving technology, particularly if cheap and flexible labour is available. I want to argue in the next section that only a minority of producers are in a position to invest in new technology as an alternative to finding ways of cheapening labour and intensifying work in order to remain profitable.

Those readers who find theoretical debates tedious may want to move on to the next chapter and accept this argument on trust. It is hoped that the evidence produced in subsequent chapters will amply illustrate its validity.

The best of both worlds for whom?

In 1981 the English language translation of Frobel, Heinrichs, and Kreye's *The New International Division of Labour* was published. The authors' basic argument is that given the constantly changing nature of the product in the clothing industry, further mechanisation of the production process is deemed too risky. Thus the continuing search for cheap labour on a global basis became the preferred strategy of West German clothing firms to combat a falling rate of profit. By 1975 the authors show that a majority of firms in the FRG had relocated an increasing share of the labour-intensive assembly stages of their production to low-wage developing countries and to Eastern Europe. Why the FRG went down the relocation route in its search for cheap labour will be discussed in Chapter 3. Suffice it to say here that the authors provide abundant evidence to show that this was the strategy pursued by a majority of manufacturers in the FRG at this time (see Frobel *et al.*, 1981).

But at a theoretical level, the basic thesis of *The New International Division of Labour* has been the subject of much critical debate. One of the main criticisms of the text is that its basic thesis tends to identify the search for cheap labour (the extraction of absolute surplus value) as capital's prime means of restoring the rate of profit, rather than identifying increasing labour productivity, principally through technical innovation (the extraction of relative surplus value) as the general basis of capital accumulation (Duffield, 1981; Jenkins, 1984).

In his critique, Jenkins argues that:

> when it is recognised that relative surplus value is the general
> basis of accumulation in the capitalist mode of production,
> relocation can be seen as a specific response which arises in
> circumstances when there are major obstacles to increasing
> relative surplus value. Thus it occurs primarily in industries
> such as electronics and clothing where economic and
> technological considerations make increased mechanisation
> difficult with existing technologies.

(Jenkins, 1984: 43)

Jenkins goes on to argue that such relocation may be temporarily limited to the extent that once the obstacles to technological innovation are overcome, such production may be redomesticated.

Needless to say in the real world we are not confronting 'capital' but 'capitals'; textile multinational alongside independent inner-city sweatshop. While the former have pursued a range of strategies available to them in their pursuit of profitability, based on technical innovation at home and the allocation of factors of production to their most efficient use at home and abroad through an international division of labour, the latter firms have little scope for independent action. The prime means of maintaining profitability amongst the small, secondary-sector firms is the extraction of surplus through the intensification and casualisation of work.

But even where there is the possibility of investment it needs to be realised that the rate of technical innovation has always been related as much to factors on the labour-supply side (such as the price and skill flexibility of the available labour force) as it has to the technical possibilities within an industry. As long as a supply of cheap and flexible labour is available to the clothing industry, then technical gradualism will prevail. The next chapter shows how the development of the women's fashionwear industry has always relied upon such a pool of cheap and flexible labour.

Chapter two

Echoes of the past?

This chapter unpacks the capital–labour relationship in the women's fashionwear industry historically and reveals a complex of gender, ethnic, and racial relations. It is suggested, therefore, that one cannot apply pure capital logic in explaining how the structure of the industry or its labour process developed, nor the character of entrepreneurship in the industry.

cond itions

When people describe the pay and conditions of workers and homeworkers labouring for contemporary sweatshops in the inner cities of London, Birmingham, Manchester, Leicester, and Coventry (to name but a few of the cities where the production of women's fashion clothing takes place) they will often remark how reminiscent such conditions are of the nineteenth century. In fact when we take a closer look at how the women's fashionwear industry developed and the reasons for its continuing location in the inner cities, we realise that the economics of the production of cheap fashion clothing has changed very little over the past 150 years.

Unpacking the historical record of women's fashionwear production is not simple, basically because the clothing industry is made up of a number of different sectors, each representing a reasonably distinct labour process that in turn represents variations in the sexual division of labour. Unfortunately, not all historical accounts of the clothing industry disaggregate between sectors, which makes the task more difficult.

Nevertheless, there is little doubt that, traditionally, London has been the fashion centre of Britain and that the location of wholesalers and an unlimited supply of cheap and flexible labour were the determining factors in the establishment of a ready-to-wear clothing industry in the East End of London in the mid-nineteenth century.

In Wray's account of the pre-war industry, she argues that up until 1900 only a small proportion of ready-to-wear clothing production was for women and this was generally undertaken by retail shop-keepers and department stores who wanted to keep their staff busy when enough 'bespoke' orders were not forthcoming (Wray, 1957: 18). In trying to trace the development of the fashionwear trade we need to concentrate on what was referred to in the nineteenth century as dressmaking.

The introduction of the sewing machine in 1846 and the band-saw in 1858 revolutionalised production methods throughout the cloth-ing industry allowing for the fragmentation of tasks and the substitu-tion of unskilled for skilled labour. Nevertheless, in London, this did not generate the move from home to factory production that was taking place in the provinces. On the contrary, Sally Alexander ar-gues in her analysis of women's work in nineteenth-century London that the introduction of the sewing machine simply revolutionalised the productivity of female waged work within the home (Alexander, 1983: 48). High rents and the cost of transporting fuel within London were major deterrents to the introduction of the factory system where the clothing industry's viability relied upon a cheap, unskilled reserve army of female and immigrant labour trapped in London's East End. Why did such a labour force exist?

The sexual division of labour

The pool of casual labour that had always existed in London was swelled after the Napoleonic Wars by growing numbers of immi-grants from Ireland and agricultural districts. As the men looked for work in building and the docks, their wives and children looked to the 'slop trades' for work (Hall, 1962: 61). The latter produced cheap goods by breaking down the skilled labour process into its semi-skilled or unskilled component parts. Alexander argues that it was the transference of the sexual division of labour from the family into social production that ensured that it was women who moved into the subordinate and auxiliary positions within those tasks (ibid.: 28). According to the dominant ideology of the nineteenth century (though it remains equally true of the late twentieth century), women's primary role was defined not as a waged worker but as an actual or potential wife and mother economically and legally de-pendent upon a male breadwinner. This has a significant impact on the conditions under which women enter and sell their labour power on the open market.

First, they enter the labour market labelled as inferior bearers of labour because they occupy a subordinate position in social relations prior to their entry into the labour market. Second, it is argued that they can be paid less than men because they are partially dependent upon sources other than their own wages for the costs of their daily and long-term reproduction (i.e. food, clothing, rent, etc., and, in the long term, periods of economic inactivity including the bearing of the next generation of workers). Third, it is within this context that men excluded women from the skilled craft guilds, so women were denied access to socially recognised skills. Fourth, while the Factory Acts passed in 1834 were seen to provide protection for women (for instance in restricting the number of hours women worked), the Acts defined women as minors and also provided a legal underpinning to the notion that a woman's rightful place was in the home caring for her husband and children (Wilson, 1977: 18). For example, Cockburn in her study of the printing unions relates how compositors met in 1886 to discuss measures to deal with the threat from women. On the one hand, the societies wanted to keep women out of the craft altogether but on the other, they had to ensure that if women did manage to gain entry their wages were brought up to the same level as men's. Sydney Webb pointed out the hypocrisy of this position given that the societies knew that no employer would give women equal pay with men given the restrictions placed on women's labour by the Factory Acts (Cockburn, 1983: 34). Finally, the demand for a family wage by organised male labour was both consistent with this exclusionary practice and could be ultimately justified as providing the material preconditions for conformity to the Victorian bourgeois family form of 'male breadwinner' and 'dependent wife' (Land, 1980).

What these processes represented is particularly well summed up by Cockburn when she suggests that:

> The struggle to keep women competitors out of work and to wrest from the employers a wage sufficient to keep an entire family may have seemed to the men at the time, as it is often represented today, a necessary class struggle, pure and simple. It was, nonetheless, also a struggle by men to assure patriarchal advantage.
>
> (Cockburn, 1983: 35)

Thus, rather than struggle for equal pay and the abolition of unnecessary restrictions on women's work, the attitude and practice of organised male labour simply compounded the notion of women as actual or potential domestic labourers and as inferior workers. In addition, exclusionary practice simply meant the confinement of women to unskilled, low-paid work and the creation of a potential reserve army of labour that could be used to undercut male workers.

Thus, in the period 1830–50, the system of sweating or subcontracting proliferated in the London clothing trade on the backs of largely female labour. Before 1832, Jews could not become City freemen and by the middle of the eighteenth century, they had established a flourishing second-hand clothes business at the City limits. It was out of these old clothes businesses that the wholesale business of ready-to-wear clothing grew. The wholesale clothier cut out cloth in stock sizes and gave out the cloth to the lowest bidding sweater who was a 'middleman'. The sweater's workshop was normally the home where he would set his wife and children to work and engage the wives and children of casual labourers in the docks and building trades. It was a process where sweaters constantly searched for the cheapest available labour in order to undercut competition (Hall, 1962; Jones, 1971; Alexander, 1983). Jones (1971) argues that the harshest effects of the introduction of the sweating system were felt by the low-skilled female homeworkers whose earnings actually fell from 5s. 9d. per week in 1848 to 3s. 2d. in 1860 (p. 109).

The 1851 Census records 125,000 women aged over 20 years in the clothing and shoemaking industries of whom 43,000 were dressmakers and milliners. Many of the latter would have received work directly from the West End fashion houses, though Alexander comments: 'The West End outworker was as exploited by the fashionable houses as the East End labourer's wife was by the showroom or warehouse, sometimes more so' (Alexander, 1983: 59).

Henry Mayhew, a nineteenth-century journalist and chronicler of the appalling conditions endured by much of London's working class at the time, tells of 18-hour working days, girls as young as 14 years of age suffering from 'indigestion in its most severe forms, disturbance of the uterine actions, palpitation of the heart, pulmonary affections threatening consumption and various affections of the eyes' (quoted in Alexander, 1983: 36). Such rapid deterioration in general health and eyesight led to the young women's movement down the scale of employment, 'where the skirts are made at home (and they) seldom work for gentlefolk, but are supported by the wives of tradesmen and mechanics' (ibid.: 36). Thus whatever the sector, women's work in the clothing industry was arduous, poorly paid, and hazardous to health.

Immigrants in the production of womenswear

The system of sweating was well established in London before the large-scale immigration of Russian and Polish Jewish refugees in 1881–6 (they were fleeing the pogroms in their homelands). This particular wave of immigration certainly intensified, but did not initiate, as many argued it did, the pernicious system of sweating that the new refugees had little choice but to enter.

Nevertheless, it was argued that Jews undercut English workers and forced the latter into casual work. A dock labourer giving evidence to the 1892 Royal Commission on Labour claimed that:

> The foreigners will not come to that work. It is too hard for them: but they go into shoe-making and tailoring and cabinet making. That is more easy and cleaner for them: and should a foreigner go in to do that to all intents and purposes an Englishman will have to step out. It is the Englishman that comes to the dock.
>
> (quoted in Jones, 1971: 110)

No recognition was given to the fact that many of the immigrants had been tailors in their homeland and that the ready-to-wear section of the clothing industry was traditionally Eastern European Jewish (Hall, 1962: 61). Thus it was only to be expected that friends, relations, and co-ethnics would enter an industry where their compatriots had already created a niche, particularly given problems of language and anti-semitism. Wray argues that most of the Jewish male immigrants were absorbed into the men's tailoring industry, but in London they also provided the basis for most of the early development of women's ready-made tailoring production (Wray: 1957: 19). Wray argues that the small Jewish-owned firms played a key role in the development of the subcontracting system. Male Jewish homeworkers in women's tailored outerwear gradually improved their position by taking contracts for the production of clothing in bulk instead of working on piece rates as homeworkers.

The interplay between the racial and sexual division of labour had by the 1920s and 1930s laid the basis of craft distinctions that Birnbaum *et al.* describe as 'influenced, to a large extent, by subjective attitudes' (1981: 22). In the interwar years the labour process in menswear production became subdivided; in the 1920s there was a mass recruitment of women to do what were then defined as semi-skilled tasks. The skilled tasks of pattern-making and cutting remained in male hands. In tailored womenswear a similar change in the labour process in the 1930s brought non-Jewish women into the sector, but with a less dramatic change in the sex ratio and with Jewish male machinists defining the work that they continued to do in the sector as skilled. Phillips and Taylor drawing on Birnbaum's work comment that:

> When in 1926 the Wages Council enforced a single basis for skill classification for the two sectors (i.e. menswear and womenswear) it was drawn up in such a way as, once again, to confirm the men machinists as skilled and the women as semi-skilled.
>
> (Phillips and Taylor, 1980: 85)

There was no technical reason for the distinction:

> it arose out of the struggle of men workers from the Russian, Jewish and Polish communities to retain their social status within the family, even when excluded by their position as immigrants from the 'skilled' jobs they might otherwise have done. Forced as they were to take on machining work usually done by women as semi-skilled, they fought to preserve their masculinity by defining their machining as skilled labour.
>
> (ibid.: 85)

By 1950 the balance between men and women in tailored womenswear was 50/50; by the 1960s, 60 per cent of machinists were women; but by the 1970s male Bangladeshi immigrants formed the largest single group of machinists in this sector.

The dress industry was quite different. Because dress material was light, machining in this sector was always considered to be 'woman's work', with pattern-making and cutting being the only preserve of skilled male labour. Many of the machinists in this sector were homeworkers and only a minority were Jewish women.

In 1920 the hundreds of small Jewish outdoor contractor firms in women's tailored outerwear formed themselves into the Master Ladies' Tailors' organisation (outdoor contractors defined by Wray as proprietors of workshops or factories employing three or more people and engaged in making up materials owned by another firm) who made up garments on a cut-make-and-trim (CMT) basis. Wray argues the same subcontracting system developed in dress production.

Looking back to the late nineteenth century and the very early twentieth century, the London School of Economics *New Survey of London Life and Labour,* published in 1930, comments on the lack of organisation on the part of both employers and employees in the dressmaking section of the clothing industry and sees this as a major factor in the establishment of Trade Boards for the clothing industry. A select parliamentary committee recommended the establishment of Trade Boards in 1907 in the hope that employment conditions in sweated industries would be improved. In 1909 a minimum statutory rate of pay was adopted and a Trade Board set up in men's tailoring. In 1919 a Trade Board was set up for Wholesale Mantles and Costumes, and in 1920 for Dressmaking and Women's Light Clothing. The principal aim of Trade Boards was to secure through statutory compulsion some of the results that organised trades produce through collective bargaining (London School of Economics, 1930: 253). The boards fixed minimum time and piece rates for workers whether they worked in factories or at home.

The development of dualism

Between 1891 and 1911 the number of women involved in dressmaking in London remained fairly constant at around 137,000 but between 1911 and 1921 there was a drop in both the numbers employed in dressmaking and the number of small employers. The 1924 census report indicated a decline in the number of homeworkers for the industry as a whole from 40,090 in 1907 to 20,035 in 1924 and Wray argues that by the late 1920s factory production of clothing was becoming the normal method of production in the clothing industry, although it was by no means universal (Wray, 1957: 22). She argues that in the 1930s dressmaking had also become a mainly factory industry. The Chief Factory Inspector's Report of 1932 claimed that homeworkers:

had become a small reserve of factory-trained workers (working mainly in homes with a high standard of comfort and cleanliness) who were called on, in times of seasonal demand, to supplement factory production; the unskilled, partially trained, homeworker, typical of the clothing industry in the early twentieth century is a thing of the past.

(ibid.: 22)

Hall also argues that the 'worst aspects' of the industry were bound to disappear as employment options for women expanded, as 'alien' immigration was restricted in 1911, as factory legislation was tightened and as the Trade Boards were introduced (Hall, 1962). Undoubtedly, all of these measures were likely to push the industry away from a complete reliance on cheap labour to an emphasis on raising the productivity of labour. In explaining the apparent drop in the number of homeworkers, Wray argues that the economies of factory production began to outweigh the previous advantage of cheapness of homework. She lists lack of close quality supervision, the cost and loss of time in transporting the work to and from the homeworker's house, and the failure of some to complete the work on time. Set against this was the increased simplicity of women's fashion and the introduction of new equipment that made factory production more efficient (and which was too specialised for use by homeworkers). In addition, the introduction of measures to protect rayon production, a subsequent expansion in its production, and a corresponding drop in price led, Wray argues, to the substitution of rayon for silk and cotton in factory production, further reducing the price of ready-made dresses (Wray, 1957: 18–26).

In my view, some of the data Wray draws her conclusions from may paint a less than complete picture of the womenswear industry. First, there has always been a huge under-renumeration of homeworkers in the industry. The 1890 House of Lords Select Committee on the Sweating System recommended that all factory occupiers keep a list of their homeworkers and these lists should be open to inspection by 'an authorised inspector' (Roxby, 1984: 138). Yet in 1921 it was claimed:

The giver-out of work must be compelled under very stringent conditions, and with very heavy penalties attached to keep an absolutely complete list of his workers. He does not do it now,

he has never done it, and he will never do it under the existing
law.

(Report of the National Conference on Sweated Industries,
Glasgow, quoted in Roxby, 1984: 136)

Wray herself admits that the small employers often failed to file their
census returns. One might also surmise that once the Trade Boards
were set up, laying down a minimum wage for indoor *and* home-
based workers, employers would be even less likely to declare their
homeworkers who in every study carried out earn less than the minimum and less than their counterparts who work in factories (for instance Crine, 1979). In short, while there is little doubt that the volume of factory production increased in the interwar period, the unpredictable nature of fashionwear production has always necessitated a flexible workforce and homeworkers constitute the near-per-
fect solution to that need. Wray is correct in arguing that there are
drawbacks to production based on the labour of homeworkers, particularly with regard to quality control. Nevertheless, in a sector
where fashion content and price rank much higher than quality and
where production costs can be slashed, homeworking remains a very
attractive option for producers.

Second, the 1939 Board of Trade inquiry into the clothing industry excluded factories employing less than 10 workers and yet 46
per cent of all establishments surveyed only had between 10 and 25
workers. In addition, 50 per cent of all production in womenswear
remained concentrated in London (Wray, 1957: 28). We know that
the vast majority of units in London employ less than 10 people, a
fact that has emerged from numerous studies and analyses of central
land-use registers (see for instance Wilkins, 1982). But this has only
been officially confirmed since the revised basis for collecting statistics on establishment size came into operation in 1985 (this under-
remuneration is discussed at length in Chapter 4).

My feeling is that while there was some shift from sweatshop to
factory production, the latter never replaced the former, much of
which became invisible at an official level in order to avoid attempts
at greater regulation of the sector. What in fact developed between
1911 and the Second World War was 'dualism' in the industry. The
development of the 'modern' factory-based firm located outside
London using increasingly sectionalised methods of assembly alongside the traditional sweatshop sector with its retinue of home-

workers based in the inner cities. This dualism persisted and became more clear-cut with post-war immigration (residentially concentrated in the inner cities).

In analysing the immediate post-war period, Wray argues that the lack of skilled labour, the cramped factory conditions, and the now high charges of CMT firms were incentives for manufacturers (that is, larger firms who usually gave out work to subcontractors) to move out of London to the development areas such as South Wales. Areas such as these had large supplies of trainable 'green' labour and special building facilities. The larger factories allowed for a reorganisation in production methods and with it a fragmentation of previously skilled tasks for sectionalised production methods (that is, replacing the method of making through).

Wray argues that the move to development areas was more attractive to dress manufacturers than to producers of women's tailored outerwear. Her explanation is that the latter required a more complicated making-up process, a heavy reliance on skilled labour, and a less standardised type of cloth. As a result a higher proportion of production and employment in tailored outerwear remained in London, particularly production at the top end of the fashion-clothing market. In contrast, dress assembly is more amenable to sectionalisation and with it the substitution of semi-skilled for skilled labour. Wray does not query the basis of these skill distinctions and the possibility that they rested on non-technical factors.

She goes on to argue that the drawbacks of the new Taylorised production methods (see p. 58) favouring stable styles with longer production runs soon became apparent. Apparently, as early as 1951 such production strategies ran into difficulties as fashion came to heavily influence demand, which in turn became less predictable (ibid.: 58).

Wray turns to Jeffreys' work on retailing to explain the survival route for such firms. As we have noted earlier, in the nineteenth century much dressmaking was related to the workshops of West End houses and later, department stores became pioneers in the ready-made production of clothing in their own workshops. Nevertheless, this involvement of department stores in the actual production of clothing did not expand in the post-war period. Fewer and fewer department stores showed any interest in manufacturing. Alongside the department stores and the independent retailers, the post-war period saw the growth of the multiple retailers, including what came to be called the variety chains such as Marks and Spencer, Littlewoods, and British Home Stores. Between 1950 and 1955, the multiple slice of the womenswear market increased from 22 per cent to 28 per cent, while the independent retailers' share fell from 53 per cent to 49 per cent (Wray, 1957: 136). Jeffreys argues that multiple retailing is 'the natural complement of the growth of standardised, larger scale production' (Jeffreys, 1954: 342). Wray's data support his argument in so far as all the relatively new dress factories in development areas in her sample relied heavily on orders from multiple-chain retailers. In contrast, production for the multiples played a much less important role for those factories producing women's tailored outerwear that were set up in the development areas. In nearly all cases, Wray found that the factories had been opened by London fashion firms with their own brand name that used advertising to secure a market for the increased output that the larger greenfield site factories provided (Wray, 1957: 240).

Wray described the dress factories as producing garments of the lower medium-quality grade with a minimum run of 1,000, though 3,000–5,000 was necessary for maximum production efficiency. Nevertheless, such factories were, by 1951, operating in a highly competitive situation and while they could secure orders for long runs from the multiples and mail order firms, they could not afford to turn away the smaller orders. The latter were subcontracted to the inner London sweatshops with their retinue of homeworkers, which had always and continued to supply a more flexible form of production (Wray, 1957: 186–92). Only two such firms were included in Wray's study but she includes 1951 census data that underlines (a) the concentration of outdoor factory production in London; 91 per cent of all work given out by principal firms went to London-based factories and (b) the important role played by outdoor contractors in the womenswear industry. Even though firms employing less than 10 people are not included in the figures, approximately a quarter to a third of all production capacity in both tailored and dress sections of womenswear is supplied by outdoor contractors. Wray emphasises that the main advantages for principal firms of using outdoor contractors is to meet seasonal fluctuations in demand and to supply short runs of different styled garments at very short notice. Repeat orders are then made for the best sellers. In short, the flexibility necessary for successful fashionwear production was and continues to be supplied by outdoor units operating on a cut-make-and-trim or make-and-trim basis.

Thus the post-war picture of the womenswear industry is the development of a dualist structure of primary (what Wray refers to as principal firms) and secondary firms (contractors). The primary firms, whether they remained in the traditional sites of production or not relied on subcontracting to meet fluctuations in demand. Nevertheless, a proportion of production capacity moved to new sites introducing long runs of standardised production with a sectionalised labour process. The labour supply in the green-field sites was described by Wray as follows: 'Most of the operatives are recruited as 15-year-old school leavers, who after training, generally work for about five years before leaving to become housewives' (Wray, 1957: 187). She says that all the factories are 'equipped with modern machinery and equipment, installed when they were opened after the war' (ibid.: 187).

Yet Wray admits that despite the obvious advantages that economies of scale were bringing to the industry, 'the largest part of the women's clothing industry is still based on London, which is the home of the small producer'. Her description of the London post-war industry is worth considering in full:

> It is here that a large number of small, inconvenient, and relatively badly equipped factories dating from pre-war days, continue to exist and even to flourish. Many of them are outdoor factories and, although there was a tendency for firms to switch from outdoor to indoor production immediately after the war, the outdoor contractor seems to have regained much of his pre-war importance in London. There are acute labour difficulties in London (as in other pre-war clothing centres) but they have been met by utilising all available sources of labour, including the post-war influx of Cypriots (many of whom are trained tailors) and Jamaicans. There are few bars of race, creed or colour in the London clothing factories. Some manufacturers notably blouse makers make good use of home workers.
>
> (Wray, 1957: 63)

Thirty years on little has changed in the London industry; the secondary sector of subcontracting firms continues to supply the flexibility necessary for profitable production in the fashion clothing industry. The structure of the industry then and now looks something like Figure 2.1. In the London industry, employers and workforce remain multi-ethnic. The 1979 Labour Force Survey indicated

---

Retailers

Most of whom have no production facilities of their own

Wholesalers
(supply retailers)

Manufacturers

Some have production facilities of their own and some do not, others retain a mere skeleton staff of pattern makers and finishers. Whatever the production capacity they supply either direct to retailers or do so through a wholesaler.

Cut-make-and-trim or make-and-trim contractors

Manufacturers usually supply textiles and patterns but subcontract production to these firms. CMT firms complete the whole production process. Make-and-trim firms simply assemble pre-cut garments. Both types of firms may have all on-site workers, no on-site workers, or a core of on-site workers and a retinue of homeworkers.

Homeworkers

Receive cut garments from either a manufacturer or a subcontractor. Homeworkers assemble the garments in their own home usually using their own equipment.

Figure 2.1 Structure of the London fashion industry

that 43 per cent of the 60,000 strong clothing workforce in London was composed of ethnic minorities, though this official figure does not take account of homeworkers (who do not have employment contracts or rarely register themselves as self-employed) or of illegal immigrants. Reports on the London clothing industry suggest that the vast majority of both entrepreneurs and labour in the London industry are drawn from ethnic minorities (Leigh *et al.* 1981: 23; GLC Economic Policy Group, 1984). In London's clothing industry 80 per cent of employment is accounted for by firms employing less than 50 people. In addition, a staggering 44 per cent of all workers in the dress section in London are homeworkers (Leigh *et al.*, 1981: 30).

A continuum, not 'echoes of the past'

We have spent a good deal of time examining the structure and functioning of the women's clothing industry up to 1950. What is important to stress here is that the system of subcontracting developed in London in the nineteenth century, remained intact in the 1950s, and has continued to supply the flexibility in production necessitated by unpredictable fashion demand. What has changed, as we shall see in later chapters, is the spatial boundaries of the subcontracting system. With increasingly easy and fast motorway links between London and the Midlands, the latter has become, since the late 1970s, an important site of subcontracted production for London-based firms.

Nevertheless, what did change significantly between the 1950s and the late 1970s was the increasing power of multiples such as Marks and Spencer and British Home Stores, etc. to dictate production requirements to the clothing industry. The immediate post-war move by some of the industry to longer runs of standardised production in large, new factories was encouraged by these retailers who wanted good quality goods at competitive prices, and fashion came a poor second. But it was precisely this strategy that led many of the same retailers (excepting Marks and Spencer) to capitalise on the new supply possibilities that began to open up in the low-wage developing countries during the 1960s. As long as fashion sensitivity was not the primary consideration, the world-market factories of Taiwan, South Korea, the Philippines, etc. could produce it more cheaply than a British factory, which paid its workers at least the statutory minimum and observed their employment and health and safety rights.

Yet, while fashionwear has not been immune to the ravages of import penetration, it has been less affected than the more highly standardised sectors of clothing production such as men's shirts. In short, while there have been closures and redundancies in the sector, international competition and recession have by no means devastated the sector. Thus, in some areas such as the West Midlands, the womenswear industry has mushroomed and provides the necessary flexibility in a sector that survives on the rapid production of unstandardised garments at prices that compete with the low-wage developing countries.

But it does remain conventional wisdom to state that the UK clothing industry is in decline and that the major source of declining

misconceptions

35

production and employment is the penetration of the domestic market by imports from low-wage countries. In the next chapter we examine the validity of this 'wisdom' and who it is that actually benefits from the export-led growth of the clothing industry in developing countries.

Chapter three

The global market place

If a company makes men's shirts or suits in Britain then the threat of cheap imports is a very real one. If a firm makes women's fashion clothes, then the picture is less clear. We are talking about the difference between an import penetration figure of 75 per cent for men's shirts compared to 28 per cent in women's fashionwear (Department of Trade and Industry, 1987). But this aggregate figure does not differentiate between cheap and any other kind of import (to do that we have to unpack those figures in terms of value), which is of some importance given that around half of Britain's imported clothes do not come from low-wage countries and are neither cheap to produce nor cheap to buy.

Producers in developing countries have a comparative advantage over those in developed countries if competitiveness is measured exclusively by price in the production of standardised garments i.e. garments like men's shirts, the basic design of which changes little from year to year (particularly as many producers in developing countries have shown themselves to be prepared to invest in the most up-to-date computer-based manufacturing equipment). But when it comes to the short runs and speed of delivery demanded by fashion retailers, coupled with accessibility to domestic cheap-labour sources, then any advantage that developing countries have over countries like Britain seems less clear cut.

The main reason why garments made in developing countries are perceived as a threat is because if we compare the cost of producing a thousand dresses in a factory in Britain, which abides by minimum wage and health and safety legislation and observes other employment rights, with the cost of producing those dresses in Sri Lanka, then the latter has an advantage. Even though both factories will be using very similar equipment, the Sri Lankan plant will have much lower labour costs but the same or even higher levels of productivity, the latter the result of intensified work and prolongation of the working day. In 1984 the worker in such a factory would have been earning around 19 pence per hour against £1.90 per hour in the UK (*Apparel International*, 1984).

In Free Trade Zones in particular, measures have also been enacted to curtail workers' rights and their freedom to organise. Thus, if competitiveness is measured by price alone, then the buyers for the big multiple retailers will go to Sri Lanka or other low-wage sites to place their orders.

There is widespread agreement in the British clothing industry that if the present quotas on imports were scrapped, the industry would be devastated. One aim of agreements such as the Multi-Fibre Agreement (MFA) (which aims to control the growth of imports from low-cost 'exporting' countries, e.g. South Korea, Sri Lanka) is to allow the advanced industrial countries time to adjust and restructure. Unlike other European governments the Conservative government that has been in power since 1979 has actually been withdrawing from, rather than intervening in, assisting British industry to restructure.

But the whole notion of 'cheap imports' needs unpacking, for the contents are often not what one might expect. Thus first, we will consider whether so-called cheap imports really are the primary cause of job loss in the clothing industries of advanced industrial countries. Second, we will consider why so many developing countries opted to spearhead their export-led growth through the clothing industry and whether this form of industrialisation brings those nations, and in particular the workers in such countries, any real benefits. Third, we will consider why manufacturers in the Federal Republic of Germany, but to a far less extent Britain, have opted to relocate the labour-intensive asssembly stages of clothing production to low-wage sites.

Unpacking imports

In 1953, 92 per cent of global production in clothing and 67 per cent of employment was concentrated in developed countries. In 1980, 75 per cent of global production was still concentrated in the developed countries but employment had slumped to 39 per cent. These figures represent the impact of four processes that challenge the conventional wisdom that cheap imports are largely responsible for job loss in the developed countries.

First, there is evidence that indicates that changes in productivity per employee are more important in reducing employment than the effects of import penetration (see Keesing and Wolf, 1980: 36 for a guide; and Cable, 1982). For instance, for every 1 per cent increase in productivity in the European clothing industry 15,000 jobs a year are lost. Since 1975 productivity in the UK clothing industry has risen by about 4 per cent per annum (Commission of the European Communities (CEC), 1981: 15). The trade-versus-productivity debate is very much ongoing and very differing conclusions can be drawn depending upon the data set used. Some of the uncertainties surrounding this debate are highlighted in the following extract from the CEC report cited above.

> This loss of jobs is mainly the result of the stagnation or even drop in Community production, coupled with the increase in productivity. Increased productivity itself is the result of both a reduction in manpower, owing to the disappearance of firms which are too weak and of the necessary rationalisation measures. However the relative importance of each of these causes and the direct or indirect influences of the penetration of imports cannot be determined because there are no direct statistics.
>
> (CEC, 1981: 15)

This implicitly recognises that the threat of imports will stimulate the drive towards increases in productivity in the developed countries. It will also play a strategic role in gaining workers' acceptance of subsequent changes in the labour process, which may be both labour-displacing and deskilling.

Second, while imports doubled between 1980 and 1986, around half of these came from developed countries, particularly the European Community. Imports from developed countries are worth more in value than the garments imported from developing countries (Hollings, 1987; Silberston, 1984). For example, Italian-made clothes, which are neither cheap to produce nor cheap to buy, come a close second to those imported from Hong Kong (see Table 3.1).

Third, so-called imports may in fact have a significant domestic component because they are 'outward processed' (OP). What this means is that design and cutting, the skilled or capital-intensive stages of production, are carried out in the developed countries and then sent to low-wage countries for the labour-intensive assembly stage, which constitutes 80 per cent of labour costs. In many countries such as the United States, OP is a strategy that bypasses the Multi-Fibre Agreement and similar restraint levels. For instance in the US under tariff item 807, producers using OP pay duty only on the value added to the garment abroad. The European Commission actively encourages the use of OP as a way of 'achieving greater competitiveness through the device of cost equalisation' (CEC, 1981: 51).

In 1975 the Frobel, Heinrichs, and Kreye study showed that the majority of West German clothing firms were using OP as a preferred production strategy. But in the UK, firms have become less heavily involved in OP because goods made up in this way count against UK quotas. Nevertheless, there is evidence in this and other studies that OP is regarded as a viable strategy by some producers,

Table 3.1 UK imports of clothing: percentage share from key sources (by value), 1987

Hong Kong	20.0
Italy	10.5
S. Korea	7.5
FRG	6.5
Portugal	6.2
Irish Rep.	4.3
India	4.1
France	3.9
Netherlands	3.1
Taiwan	2.9
Israel	2.6
Greece	2.4
Turkey	2.2
Bel/Lux	2.1
Thailand	1.8
China	1.5
Austria	1.2
Philippines	1.2
Cyprus	1.2
Singapore	1.1
Pakistan	1.0
USA	0.8
Denmark	0.8
Spain	0.5

Source: British Business (1988): 26 August, p.3.

particularly through using those countries bordering on or in the Mediterranean, which have a preferential trading agreement with the EEC, for example, Cyprus. This agreement allows garments made up in those countries from fabric woven or knitted either in the EEC or in the exporting country to enter the EEC duty-free.

In 1983 the *Observer* newspaper reported that a British company, Wearwell, based in London's East End and headed by Turkish-Cypriot millionaire Asil Nadir was shipping out 15,000 ready-cut women's and girls' dresses per week to Cyprus for assembly by 500 to 1,000 homeworkers. The dresses were sent back to London for finishing and then exported mainly to Arab countries. The company whose profits in 1982 were £4,200,000 and which had twice received the Queen's Award for Exports, was paying the homeworkers 22p per dress (the *Observer*, 24 April 1983: 2).

Manufacturers may also switch their OP from country to country in line with the expansion or contraction of quotas in MFA re-negotiations and according to wages. For workers in a country such as the Philippines, where two-thirds of all clothing exports are in fact outward-processed goods, a relocation of production by one or two of the multinational manufacturers can mean redundancy and unemployment. Clothing industries in the low-wage countries, which are heavily dependent upon outward processing, are, as we shall see below, in a precarious position.

The clothing unions in Britain have in the past been opposed to the use of OP by British firms, arguing that it constitutes the direct export of jobs. In the same way, firms whose production is wholly based in the developed countries regard outward processing as unfair competition and it is they who shouted loudest in the call for increased protectionism. OP is not the only way in which manufacturers are involved in overseas production. As retailers began to source in the low-wage countries in the 1960s some manufacturers adopted the 'if you can't beat them join them' strategy lest they be bypassed altogether by the retailers. Nearly all the vertically integrated textile firms such as Tootals, Courtaulds, Coats Viyella, and some of the large independent manufacturers have directly invested in overseas production facilities. Much of this production is destined for overseas markets but some manufacturers are producing solely for the UK market.

Reporting on the Coats Viyella fall of pre-tax profits from £81m to £76m for the first half of 1988, in an article entitled 'Coats Viyella is put through the mill', the *Financial Times* states:

> Coats is now rationalising home production in favour of
> sourcing overseas, like the US and West German textile giants.
> ... Clothing is one of the chief candidates for overseas
> sourcing. Coats expanded its sourcing in Hong Kong earlier this
> year by buying a sizeable export house and it is keen to establish
> similar operations in other countries. ... Imports seem certain
> to rise.
>
> (*Financial Times,* 23 September 1988: 21)

The advantages of siting production for the home market in low
wage countries is obvious, particularly if production is located in one
of the numerous free trade zones. For instance in December 1982,
machinists in one Philippines-based subsidiary of a British clothing
firm were earning approximately £7 for a 40-hour week after deductions (Kasama, 1983). Factories are sometimes jointly owned by indigenous capitalists and the overseas customer (Tang, 1980). In
other cases premises are merely leased. On a personal visit to the
New Economic Zone in Shenzen province, Southern China in
January 1989, I established that clothing workers were earning as
little as £80–£100 a month in the export processing factories.

The final point we need to consider on the question of imports is
the role of the retailer, because at the end of the day it is the highly
centralised buying power of the big retailers that has a controlling
influence on where garments are produced and purchased from.

In 1984 I obtained information on sourcing from the major
multiple and variety chain stores (except C&A) and the largest mail
order company in the UK. The most important fact to emerge was
that they all claimed to source at least 60 per cent of their orders in
the UK. In 3 cases, the retailers had increased overseas sourcing
within the last 5 years and in 4 cases, the retailers had decreased their
overseas sourcing (unfortunately precise figures cannot be given for
reasons of non-comparability between returns). While a large number of developing countries were listed by the retailers, all also
mentioned Italy. Since 1984 we know that Burtons has further reduced its overseas sourcing, M & S continues to source 90 per cent
in the UK, and Next sources well over 80 per cent.

Thus, while many of the retailers are seeing advantages in sourcing an even larger chunk of their orders in Britain, in 1984 at least,
not all were doing so and competition to British-produced goods

from Italy, an advanced industrial society, was marked. As we shall see later in the case of garments made in Thailand, retailers can expect a retail mark-up on ex-factory costs of 200–300 per cent, whereas Marks and Spencer's mark-ups on British-produced goods are nearer 70 per cent.

But the debate about cheap imports is not in fact about developing countries 'dumping' their goods on the markets of the advanced industrial countries. It is retailers who buy garments in low-wage labour sites abroad because they can have a bigger mark-up without, in many cases, any regard to the wages, conditions, and rights of the workers who produce them. We consider the dubious benefits that clothing industrialisation has brought to developing countries in the next section.

Hong Kong and east–west trade in clothing

Hong Kong became a British colony in 1841 and the centre for import–export business between China and the West. When Japan invaded China in 1938, 500,000 refugees fled to Hong Kong, including textile capitalists. When Mao's Communist Party took over the reins of government in China in 1949, this exodus of refugee capital and labour continued and a new factory-based textile industry was established in Hong Kong that was able to plug in to the existing East–West trading networks.

It was precisely at this time that British retailers began the search for cheap garments abroad and as a member of the Commonwealth, Hong Kong enjoyed preferential import tariff arrangements. As late as 1962 Hong Kong was the only significant exporter of clothing among the developing countries (Keesing and Wolf, 1980: 13). In terms of value, clothing imports from Hong Kong continue to outstrip those of any other producer on the British market. Textiles and clothing imports from Hong Kong have long been regarded as a threat to the British industry and as such voluntary export restraint levels agreed to in 1959 became translated and extended into the Multi-Fibre Agreement in 1973 covering textile trade as a whole between developed and developing countries.

The MFA supposedly encourages trade liberalisation while safeguarding signatory state industries against the disruptive effects that such action might have. A principal stated aim of the agreement is to encourage the growth of the textile and clothing industries in the developing countries (Silbertson, 1984). Nevertheless, there is plenty of evidence to suggest that the MFA may in fact seriously distort the growth of developing countries. The United Nations Conference on Trade and Development (UNCTAD) argues that:

> Textiles and clothing is the engine of growth for many developing countries. Market contraction resulting from protectionist measures causes serious balance-of-payments problems, misallocation of resources and a debt-servicing burden which reduces these countries' capability to import from the developed countries.
>
> (International Labour Organization (ILO), 1987: 5)

Big producers such as Hong Kong, South Korea, and Taiwan have been hardest hit by MFA quotas that have favoured the less developed countries. This has had a number of outcomes. First, in conjunction with a tendency to wage-cost inflation in the 'Big Three', there has been a drive to upgrade production. MFA quotas are set by volume, not by value (ILO, 1987: 9). Second, producers in Hong Kong have not been slow to switch to perceiving raising labour productivity as a method of sustaining profitability given the demise of cheap labour. By the end of 1985, 20 clothing firms in Hong Kong had invested in the Gerber computerised apparel system (Chisolm *et al.*, 1986: 41). Finally, in the case of Hong Kong, this strategy has been combined with some relocation of production to other countries, using outward processing or acting as middlemen in sending orders for cheap clothing to other Southeast Asian countries that have minimal or no quota restrictions (Cavanagh, 1982: 71). There was plenty of evidence to show that Hong Kong producers were simply shifting their production over the border into the New Economic Zone in Shenzen, China, when I visited in 1989. In addition, Levi jeans had scaled down their Hong Kong plants and also had moved into southern China.

Hong Kong producers have even set up factories in Britain in order to circumvent the restrictions on exporting to the US and because female wages in the northeast of England are low and labour compliant, given the staggeringly high levels of male unemployment in the region (*Business Week,* 26 August 1985: 45).

Nevertheless the Big Three as 'quota refugees' have been more likely to move to other Southeast Asian countries, such as the Philippines and more recently China, to fill up their quotas and take advantage of its cheaper labour (Paglaban, 1978: 6; information collected during author's personal visit).

Creating cheap labour

As more and more developing countries have been forced to follow the export-oriented route to growth (as opposed to import substitution, which ran up against the problems of small internal markets), so competition between countries for the sourcing favours of the chain retailers and giant multinational manufacturers such as Levi Strauss increases.

In the late 1960s and early 1970s, countries such as the Philippines endeavoured to attract foreign manufacturing investment by setting up Free Trade Zones (FTZs). For example, in 1973 the Philippines Bataan Export Processing Zone was completed offering permission for 100 per cent foreign ownership, exemption from payment of municipal, provincial, and export taxes and tax-free and duty-free importation of raw materials, machinery, and equipment (Paglaban, 1978: 7). In the Philippines (and most other countries) 90 per cent of garment workers are women. Many migrate from rural areas and are housed in boarding houses, sometimes eight to a room. Paglaban, following Samir Amin, argues that such large rural reserves of labour in underdeveloped countries such as the Philippines serve two main functions for the capitalist sector in the same countries.

First, because they remain with one foot in the subsistence sector, the rural reserves shoulder a large part of the reproductory costs of the capitalist sector. The subsistence sector has borne all the costs of rearing the worker and in old age or periods of unemployment he or she can return to the rural area. (The benefits are directly analogous to those that accrue to the advanced industrial countries from international labour migration.) In addition, Paglaban argues that rice prices are kept artificially low by the government, further subsidising firms in the capitalist sector by reducing subsistence costs and therefore helping keep wages low at the expense of the rice farmers. The other main function of the subsistence sector is to continuously supply the capitalist sector with more 'willing' workers than it can actually absorb – willing in the sense that they are compelled to migrate through the decomposition of the subsistence sector, largely through dispossession, the inroads of capitalist agribusiness, and the penetration of the cash economy (Phizacklea, 1983: 7). As the

45

relative surplus population is driven into town to find waged work, it exerts a downward pressure on the wages of those already in employment. In addition, the knowledge that there are other migrant workers who can be substituted for the same job acts as a powerful deterrent to worker organisation against oppression and exploitation in what have come to be called world-market factories.

But the fact that these workforces are almost wholly female is not coincidental. We have already examined the factors that make women a highly attractive form of labour power for the capitalist sector (see Chapter 2). Women are paid less than men because it is always assumed that they are working for 'pin money' and are partially dependent upon sources other than their own wages for the costs of their reproduction. Such assumptions do not of course have any bearing on how long or how hard women might be expected to work. Women in Sri Lankan Free Trade Zones speak of:

> A quantum such as is impossible for a female worker to deliver in an hour, is always targeted. Fines are imposed when such quantity is not delivered on time. We are made to work even outside working hours. Even a beast will know whether it is possible to work continuously for 12 hours in the same posture seated on a four-legged stool.

> (*Voice of Women*, 1982)

The same women speak of 'all that we have to anticipate in the long run is to possess a debilitated and emaciated body, after exhausting what is earned where it is earned' (ibid). In short, wages are only sufficient for the day-to-day reproduction of labour power, nothing more. Similar harrowing evidence of the wages and conditions experienced by women workers in world-market factories in Bangkok, Thailand were revealed in Granada Television's 'World in Action' (6 February 1984). The workers were young girls, some only 12 years of age, who sewed garments from 8 a.m. until 11 p.m. at night, 7 days a week. If production targets were not met, then they were made to work all night. The girls slept in the factories (no beds were supplied) and in one factory at least, they were locked in. Rice was their staple diet. Experienced machinists earned less than £30 per month. Orders were placed with these world-market sweatshops by British firms including Great Universal Stores, Littlewoods, C&A, Debenhams, and Woolworths. The programme showed a jumpsuit ex-factory costing £4.65 that was offered in the GUS catalogue for £15. 99. The retail price was similar to British-produced goods so the savings of overseas sourcing went to the retailer in the form of profit rather than to the customer.

When asked to justify such sourcing policies after the programme, a spokesperson from Debenhams responded:

> But we have not placed orders from Thailand directly ... we merely work to sealed samples placing orders through buying agents who then go out and get them made up, that's the only thing we are interested in. Providing the merchandise measures up to the sealed sample we are not concerned about sources.
>
> (*Drapers Record,* 11 February 1984: 5)

But there are other built-in advantages of employing women for painstaking, labour-intensive work that carries with it a socially constructed label of 'unskilled' and therefore badly paid work. As Elson and Pearson have argued the so-called 'nimble fingers' that women possess are not inherited; they are a result of 'the training they have received from their mothers and other female kin since early infancy in the tasks socially appropriate to a woman's role' (Elson and Pearson, 1981: 92). Sewing is such a skill used in sweatshops throughout the world and also provides skills transferable to other assembly operations. But this childhood training is invisible and remains undervalued because it is a part of women's work within the traditional domestic sexual division of labour. What this means when women's skills are transferred to the capitalist labour process is aptly summed up by Elson and Pearson: 'To a large extent women do not do "unskilled" jobs because they are the bearers of inferior labour; rather the jobs they do are "unskilled" because women enter them already determined as inferior bearers of labour' (ibid.: 93).

The fact that women come to the capitalist labour process already trained in this respect obviously has huge advantages for employers: 'It takes six weeks to teach industrial garment making to girls who already know how to sew' (Sharpston, 1975: 105). Thus whether the women are machinists in a world-market factory in Sri Lanka or a green-field site in the UK, or a sweatshop in London, their skills acquired over many years will neither be recognised as such in terms of skill classifications nor appropriately rewarded.

In the developing countries women in world-market factories are rewarded with even less than their factory-based sisters in the advanced industrial countries (though it will be pointed out in a later chapter, not necessarily less than homeworkers in the UK). But as already discussed, there are other incentives for advanced industrial producers to relocate part or all of their production to off-shore sites, particularly to FTZs.

Questioning the new international division of labour orthodoxy

Nevertheless, the extent to which relocation has been used by clothing manufacturers (as opposed to retailers sourcing their orders abroad) as a strategy to maintain profitability has been highly variable nationally. The Frobel, Heinrichs, and Kreye study referred to earlier indicated that by 1975 a majority of West German textile and garment firms had relocated a part, usually the assembly stage, or the whole of the production process to low-wage sites. They argued that this was due mainly to increasing difficulties in securing and maintaining large profits because of the cost and strength of indigenous labour and to the fact that a constantly changing product made investment in labour-saving technology too risky (1981).

There is little doubt that by the late 1960s the British and West German clothing industries were faced with virtually identical problems of declining international competitiveness. Both were large employers of immigrant female labour – in 1969, 12 per cent in the FRG and in Britain up to 30 per cent in traditional areas of clothing production such as London (Phizacklea, 1983).

In an industry that has remained technologically static since the nineteenth century, increasing labour productivity through technical innovation appears to make good sense if producers in advanced industrial societies are to restore international competitiveness. But received wisdom in the industry was that given the limpness of the material involved and, particularly in fashionwear, an ever-changing product, huge obstacles existed to the further mechanisation of production. Certainly increases in productivity were sought and continued to be achieved through work reorganisation, changes in payment systems, and minor technical changes in the production process.

Thus, technical innovation is related as much to labour-supply side factors as it is to the technical possibilities within an industry. As long as skilled but cheap and flexible labour power is available, gradualism will prevail. So for producers in Britain and the FRG, a combined strategy of technological gradualism and a continuing search for cheap labour was pursued in an attempt to restore international competitiveness.

In both countries cheaper labour was found through subcontracting production, yet the way in which the two countries pursued that strategy was markedly different. In Britain, clothing manufacturers off-loaded their high-risk, unpredictable sectors of demand (fashion clothes) and maintained flexibility by increased subcontracting domestically to the many small, inner-city firms dominated by ethnic entrepreneurs and labour (Morokvasic *et al.*, 1986; Mitter, 1986). In contrast, in the FRG, manufacturers began to exploit the labour-cost advantages of the new international division of labour by subcontracting work externally to low-wage countries (Frobel, Heinrichs, and Kreye, 1981) and by importing a high proportion of fashion goods from Italy (GATT (General Agreement on Tariffs and Trade), 1984).

Explanations for these differences lie in three main areas: the first rests with trade policy. In the post-war period, the FRG has favoured the liberalisation of trade policy and with it an acceptance of the new international division of labour between developed and developing countries, while Britain has in principle shifted under Thatcher from a protectionist to a free trade position and in practice from an interventionist to a non-interventionist policy on the domestic front (Morokvasic *et al.*, 1986). In addition, the TUC in Britain has consistently backed the clothing unions' claim that the practice of OP amounts to the direct export of jobs.

The second factor that needs to be considered is that the FRG simply did not have a secondary sector of small subcontracting firms to resort to in providing the necessary flexibility. Berlin was the traditional centre of a Jewish-dominated clothing industry. The decimation of that industry in the 1930s and the geographical isolation of Berlin after the Second World War spelt the end of the old German clothing industry. A new industry based on high-productivity, large-scale factory production took its place in Northrhine-Westphalia and Bavaria (see Morokvasic *et al.*, 1986). It was precisely to these factories that migrant women from the European periphery were recruited in the 1960s who by 1975 were becoming increasingly surplus to requirements as clothing firms had found even cheaper sources of labour in Eastern Europe and further afield.

The third and related factor lies in differing immigration policies. The FRG recruited migrant workers for specific jobs for which they were issued specific types of work and residence permits, the latter generally stating that the holder was not permitted to set up independently. In addition, until very recently family reunion was positively discouraged amongst the migrant population. What we have learnt from the historical record is that without recourse to family labour, the establishment of immigrant businesses is unlikely to take place (Bonacich and Modell, 1980). Access to unpaid or cheap and flexible labour is one of the few competitive advantages available to immigrant entrepreneurs. There are therefore structural and legal obstacles (though not insurmountable, for instance, a German 'strawperson' can be used to front a company) to the formation of an immigrant-dominated secondary sector.

The situation in Britain has of course been quite different. Migrants from the New Commonwealth not only had the right to live and work in Britain until 1962, but in most cases it has been possible for spouses and dependants to subsequently join those workers already in the UK and to enjoy the same freedom of access to the labour market. Nevertheless, while the vast majority of women are confined to certain sectors of the labour market because they are women, ethnic-minority women have also had to face racism and racial discrimination in British labour markets (Brown, 1984).

As work in the formal economy contracted, many minority workers found work in what is often referred to as the 'ethnic economy'. Self-employment became an escape route for ethnic-minority men from the drudgery of dead-end manual jobs and, more recently, unemployment. Entrepreneurial projects include small-scale manufacturing (clothing being the most important), service, and retail outlets. Such projects have low entry barriers and are highly labour-intensive and rely on the cheap or unpaid labour of mainly female relatives or friends. These projects are seen to create alternative employment structures for women shaken out of manufacturing or for those who perceive obstacles to working outside a 'safe' environment for language or cultural/religious reasons.

The ease with which anyone can set up in the clothing industry is summed up by a statement from the Clothing Economic Development Council:

> The garment industry has for the last century been dominated
> by the sewing machine which is a relatively simple, cheap and
> long-lived tool. As a result, entry to the industry has been, and

still is, easy; a few hundred pounds of capital being sufficient to purchase second-hand machines and the necessary raw materials, and to make profits if a market could be found. Even the last requirement has been relatively easy to meet because of the diversity of products demanded of the industry.

(NEDO, 1971: 6)

In short, a small redundancy payment is enough to set oneself up in business and the most important niche to be filled is cheap women's fashionwear, the end of the market where looks outweigh quality; fashion at prices most women can afford. As will be discussed in later chapters some entrepreneurs do not even bother to buy sewing machines, relying entirely upon homeworkers to assemble the garments on their own machines. Many of the homeworkers were receiving, in 1988, under 50p for 'making through' a garment, even though a large proportion of these women have built up skill and high speeds working in factories. (Ironically in the case of a woman I interviewed in Birmingham, her high speeds and deftness had been learnt from 8 years' experience in a world-market factory in India.) Within the trade it is estimated that imported goods must be at least 20 per cent cheaper than domestically produced goods if retailers are to buy or subcontract abroad. Thus we have in these very low labour costs one simple factor in explaining any expansion of domestic subcontracting. If we add to this the speed with which deliveries can and are made to the high street retailers, the growing dissatisfaction expressed by some retailers with delays, quality control, fluctuations in exchange rates, and having to finance stock in transit, then there is a real competitive advantage over producers in developing countries in the less standardised lines.

The Third World comes home

We are suggesting, therefore, that the problem of low wages and poor working conditions in the clothing industry is not confined to the developing countries. The rundown of the Wages Inspectorate since 1979 and an overstretched Health and Safety Executive are just two of the symptoms of a government attitude of turning a blind eye to sweatshop conditions in Britain today. The Third World analogy is of course not new. Commenting on the clothing industry in Hackney, Paul Harrison rightly points out that instead of competing with

Third World producers, producers in Britain should head up market to higher value-added products and invest in more productive machinery:

> But instead of shifting their terrain, many manufacturers are competing with the Third World on the Third World's own ground, by reducing real wages to not better than Hong Kong levels. If the unions were stronger in this sector and if wage rates were higher, employers would be under greater pressure to invest in new machinery or move into more profitable lines. The assault on union power, the constant calls from Conservative Party ministers for stagnant or falling real wages, would lead to Britain becoming an economy specialising in labour-intensive manufactures. This is creeping underdevelopment, in which parts of the country regress towards an economy of coolie labour, the creation of a Third World country in our midst.
>
> (Harrison, 1983: 70)

While Harrison acknowledges that the entrepreneurs in question may be: 'as much exploited by those above them in the pyramid, as exploiting those below', he needs also to acknowledge that this type of entrepreneurship is a disguised form of unemployment with meagre profit margins and little or no capital investment. If such firms are to be upgraded, they will need substantial inputs of capital and technological assistance.

But alongside the great mass of tiny firms operating with equipment that has hardly changed in the last 150 years there is a profitable sector of the industry that produces fashion garments using state-of-the-art equipment. It is to this other face of the industry that we now turn.

Chapter four

Old tech, new tech, no sweat?

I want to suggest that the UK fashionwear industry represents a dual form of industrial structure much more clearly differentiated in terms of product market and capital–labour ratios than anything we have witnessed since factory production supposedly became more profitable than production based in the home. Following Piore (1979 and Piore, 1981), it is posited that much demand in the clothing industry can be effectively separated into stable and unstable portions with a slim band of primary-sector firms using increasingly capital-intensive techniques to meet the more predictable sector of demand (predictable in the sense that many of these firms have forged a close relationship with one or two major chain retailers). Secondary-sector firms located in a largely precarious subcontractual position cater for the less predictable, cheap, and high-fashion sector of demand. Many such firms are undercapitalised, investment in productivity-enhancing equipment well beyond their means. Yet there is good evidence to suggest that firms operating under such conditions compete on price and speed with Third World producers (West Midlands Low Pay Unit, 1984; see also Chapter 6, this volume).

These two sectors are sometimes (though as we shall see by no means always) linked by a complex web of subcontracting that reduces the rigidities found in the primary sector. The dualism in this structure is reflected in technology, markets, working conditions, to a large extent an ethnic division of labour, and to some extent firm size. The 1985 *Euromonitor Report* supports this view:

> For a variety of reasons of a historical, economic and social character there has come into being in some parts of the UK a

new type of clothing industry alongside the established large firms separated from it in terms of the scale of enterprises, markets served and employment practices. Clothing has become a key area for the modern type of entrepreneurial practice encouraged in current economic policy.

(*Euromonitor*, 1985: 47)

Up until 1985 official statistics underestimated the number of small firms in the women's fashionwear sector because firms employing less than 20 people were exempt from Business Statistics Office enquiries. Estimates were made only for firms employing less than 20 persons. Those of us doing field research in the clothing industry repeatedly pointed out the huge underrenumeration of production and employment that this situation led to (see Morokvasic *et al.*, 1986; West Midlands Low Pay Unit, 1984). Since 1985 the statistics on establishment size have been collected on the basis of (a) VAT returns analysed by turnover; and (b) the inclusion of local units with less than 20 employed persons. Each local unit (site or factory) is linked to its parent VAT legal unit. The local units are analysed down to activity-heading level, for example, women's light outerwear. Thus the picture we now have of the sector is a good deal more accurate and transforms any previous description of structure. We can see from Table 4.1, using the old basis for collecting statistics on firm size, it was estimated that in 1979 there was a total of 1,707 firms in the women's light outerwear sector. Using the new basis for analysing firm size, there were 3,172 firms with less than 10 employees in women's light outerwear alone in 1987 (*PA 1003, Size Analyses of*

Table 4.1 Women's and girls' light outerwear, lingerie, and infants' wear

Local units by size	1–9	10–19	20–49	50–99	100–199	200–499	500–999	1000+	Total
1979	–	667	586	231	141	74	8	–	1,707
1985	3,220	558	339	199	124	71	8	–	4,519
1987	3,172	444	401	159	119	72	8	1	4,376
Employment									
1979	–	9,606	17,742	16,099	18,843	21,195	5,623	–	89,108
1985	13,538	7,589	10,188	13,935	17,333	19,642	4,982		87,207
1987	11,846	6,058	11,900	10,841	16,762	21,285	4,997	1,025	84,714

Source: Business Monitor, PA 1003, Size Analyses of UK Businesses, Business Statistics Office, 1979, 1985, 1987.

UK Businesses, 1987). Of all units in the women's fashionwear sector, 72 per cent employed less than 10 people in 1987. Comparing firm size over the period 1979 to 1987 it is clear that it is firms employing between 20 and 100 people that have been hardest hit in the highly competitive conditions that have existed since 1979 (though between 1985 and 1987 there was an increase in firms employing 20–49 persons). While we can say little about the number of small firms before 1985, all the research evidence testifies to their bouyancy in the post-1979 recessionary period. The 1985 *Euromonitor Report* on the UK clothing industry argued that:

> According to the Census of Production data the number of firms engaged in the made-up clothing, hats, and gloves sectors has declined quite sharply in recent years. The recent emergence of significant public concern about the number of small firms operating in the clothing sector whilst ignoring minimum wage and safety regulations leads us to suspect however that the fall may be overstated.
>
> (*Euromonitor,* 1985: 23)

Thus what appears to be the case is that the very small (under 10) and the large (over 200) have been most likely to weather what have been hard times for the British clothing industry. What we can't decipher from the establishment-size analysis is how many firms have no registered employees at all. The same form of analysis in France reveals for instance that out of 29,977 plants, 19,541 have no employees at all (see Morokvasic *et al.*, 1986). These firms include 'manufacturers' without their own production facilities who act as middlemen between the retailers and subcontractors. It also includes subcontractors who operate only with so-called self-employed workers or homeworkers with whom there is no contractual relationship.

Thus, while there are still problems with the official statistics, the revised basis for collecting statistics on establishment size is a big improvement and gives us a clearer picture of structure and restructuring in the women's fashionwear sector of the industry.

In the clothing industry, what I will refer to as a primary-sector firm is not necessarily a large unit in terms of employment size; rather it is more likely that it will be part of a multiplant enterprise affiliated to one of the vertically integrated textile giants such as Courtaulds, Tootals, or Coats Viyella (it should be emphasised that the Big Three textile groupings are responsible for a much smaller proportion of total sales in this sector than in any other branch of the clothing industry); or alternatively an independent firm of medium size (in the clothing industry medium size could be as low as 100 employees) with a stable contract relationship with one of the chain retailers. Basically we are talking about firms who are in a position to invest £120,000 in computer-aided design (CAD) equipment and a further £300,000 in computer-aided cutting equipment. In 1979 a survey carried out by NEDO indicated that firms who had invested in new technology had a turnover of at least £31m, employed in excess of 250 people, and were involved in long runs of more than one week's duration (NEDO, 1979). Certainly these were precisely the types of firm that Hoffman and Rush report being targeted at that time by the manufacturers of such equipment. The French firm, Laser Lectra, have subsequently entered the international market with a cheaper and less sophisticated system targeted at the small and medium-sized firm. In a sample of 40 Laser Lectra purchasers, establishment size ranged from 20 to 2,500 employees (Hoffman and Rush, 1983, Section 4.15). In 1983 Cockburn estimated that 60 firms throughout the British clothing industry had invested in computer-aided design and by 1988 it was estimated by the British Apparel Association that the vast majority of primary-sector firms in fashionwear were using CAD. Nevertheless the rate of diffusion throughout such a sector as women's fashionwear is of course difficult to gauge. Hoffman and Rush warn of generalising from trade estimates of diffusion based on 'large' firms because 'classifying only large firms as the total market does obviously distort the picture since it excludes the large majority of very much smaller firms' (Hoffman and Rush, 1983: 4.8). Suffice it to say here that given the kind of outlay we are talking about, the vast majority of secondary-sector firms will only get access to computer-aided design and cutting through shared bureau facilities or other forms of collective provision. What the benefits are of using these new forms of equipment and what the implications are for employment constitute the issues to be discussed in the remainder of this chapter.

How the production process in women's light outerwear has developed over the last 150 years is considered first, followed by an evaluation of the impact of new technology in the pre-assembly stages of clothing production.

Increasing labour productivity

Writing of the clothing industry in the early 1860s Marx argues that:

> At last the critical point was reached. The basis of the old method, sheer brutality in the exploitation of the workpeople, accompanied more or less by a systematic division of labour, no longer sufficed for the extending markets and for the still more rapidly extending competition of the capitalists. The decisively revolutionary machine ... is the sewing machine.
>
> (Marx, *Capital*, 1977, vol. 1: 443)

Major leaps in productivity are normally only achievable through technical innovation yet since the sewing machine was introduced in Britain in 1851, little has changed for the majority of firms within an industry with one of the lowest capital–labour ratios in manufacturing as a whole. The type of productivity leap necessary to ward off international competition bypasses much of the industry because firms are unwilling or unable to invest in the range of micro-electronically related equipment now available on the market. But according to information provided by the British Apparel Association in late 1988, the diffusion of new technology in the small band of primary-sector firms in the UK is now widespread and Courtaulds (the vertically integrated textile giant and the parent company for many of the larger clothing plants) has contributed half of a £2.5m EEC-backed BRITE (Basic Research in Industrial Technologies for Europe) research programme, examining the application of flexible manufacturing systems for the clothing industry.

A study carried out in the early 1980s indicated that digital computer and microprocessor-based innovations at the pre-assembly stage of production, that is designing, pattern-making, grading, marker-making, and cutting have raised capital intensity to 100 times that of the assembly stage (Hoffman and Rush, 1983).

The nature of the material being handled, basically its limpness, has to date proved an obstacle to further automation of the assembly stage of garment production which constitutes 80 per cent of labour costs and around 30–40 per cent of total costs.

Nevertheless, increasing labour productivity even in the largest firms depended until very recently on work reorganisation, payment systems, and piecemeal technical innovation. In my whistle-stop journey through the history of the clothing industry, it was pointed out how dressmaking as opposed to women's tailored outerwear was more amenable to sectionalised production and subsequently to the move to development area sites with green but easily trainable labour.

The Babbage Principle of an increased division of labour allowing for the substitution of what is classified as semi-skilled and unskilled labour for skilled labour was developed as a managerial strategy by Frederick Taylor and is now commonly referred to as Taylorism. Taylorist production methods were adopted throughout the new large and the majority of medium-sized firms in the sector in the immediate post-war period. It involved reorganising work at the assembly stage so that what had previously been considered skilled tasks were replaced by operations classified as semi-skilled or unskilled. These are the jobs that women do, while the remaining areas of skilled work such as design and cutting monopolised by men and commanding higher rates of pay became the focus for computerisation from the 1970s onwards.

But the move to sectionalised assembly was suited to the higher volume, more standardised runs for the big chain retailers. Operatives may only be trained for one kind of task at which they can achieve high speeds; they are not trained to switch flexibly from one task to another. In contrast the situation in many of the small inner-city firms remains largely unchanged at the assembly stage with one worker sewing a complete garment, what is called 'making through'. It is suggested that the retention of this arrangement in small firms allows for flexibility when a firm is usually involved in the production of a number of different lines at the same time. What we are witnessing here, therefore, is not just a differential range of skills amongst operatives within the production of fashion clothing, but also differences that roughly represent an ethnic division of labour. In the past when primary-sector firms have complained about the shortage of skilled labour, they are talking about operatives who can work at very high speeds on sectionalised work. This of course is changing, as flexibility is now expected of machinists in line with changing patterns of demand for short runs and varied styles. In the secondary sector (where the workforce is made up predominantly of ethnic-minority women) the ability to make through a garment from beginning to end demands a different kind of skill. Yet in neither case is the skill rewarded commensurately.

Thus, in those firms using sectionalised production practices, increases in the productivity of labour at the assembly stage have been achieved by a system of payment by results for assembly workers. Earnings are linked to measured time standards that are calculated in the following way: the task is broken down into elements; a stopwatch is used to obtain times for each element (for instance, pick up work, match pieces, sew seam, etc.); usable cycle times for each element are averaged; and an operator's performance is rated against a 'normal' pace in this way. The standard allowable time for a given unit of work is calculated and piece rates fixed. Each operator will receive a bundle of work on which is attached a ticket telling the operator at what speed she could be expected to perform that task. Angela Coyle argues that 'Most operations have a cycle time of under one minute. High productivity is essential but for the women concerned it can mean "sweating golfballs" and still not being able to reach management's production targets' (Coyle, 1982: 14). Sallie Westwood reports a similar intensification of work in her analysis of a hosiery factory in the East Midlands (Westwood, 1984). Coyle also argues that 'the ability to work at high speeds is a skill inadvertently created by deskilling. It is informally recognised as such through the particularly long training period for some operations, yet it is not explicitly acknowledged through gradings or wages' (Coyle, 1982: 15–16).

Also, until the more recent technological innovations in the pre-assembly stage, productivity improvements tended to be limited to incremental changes in machinery (such as the incorporation of minor production aids to the general sewing machine). In Britain, labour costs are low compared to many of our OECD competitors and this reinforces an attitude of technological gradualism (see Table 4.2). Women make up 80 per cent of the labour force but earn only 83 per cent of the average for manufacturing. The pace and diffusion of technical innovation will be heavily influenced by the price and skill flexibility of the available labour force. And there is a certain paradox here. One of a number of conventional wisdoms in the clothing industry is that it suffers from endemic labour shortages; yet in 1982, the last year that the Department of Employment published unemployment figures by industry, there were 46,081 unemployed clothing workers (12,825 of whom were in the women's-light-outerwear sector) chasing 2,723 vacancies in the industry as a whole (*Hollings Apparel Industry Review*, 1984).

Table 4.2 International variations in wage costs per direct employee

Country	Hourly wages incl. piecework incentive		Social costs	Wage costs Total per hour	
	£	DM	%	£	DM
West Germany	2.75	11.00	70	4.68	18.70
Egypt	0.48	1.92	52	0.73	2.92
England	1.90	7.60	27	2.41	9.25
Greece	1.21	4.85	85	2.24	8.97
Hong Kong	0.83	3.30	29	1.07	4.26
Haiti	0.30	1.19	32	0.39	1.57
Ireland	1.49	5.95	27	1.89	7.56
Italy	2.18	8.70	105	4.46	17.84
Ivory Coast	0.48	1.90	80	0.86	3.42
Malta	1.50	6.00	25	1.88	7.50
Morocco	0.30	1.20	10	0.33	1.32
Portugal	0.68	2.70	25	0.84	3.37
Spain	1.50	6.02	42	2.14	8.55
Sri Lanka	0.19	0.76	25.8	0.24	8.55
Switzerland	3.38	13.53	40	4.74	18.94
Tunisia	0.40	1.58	19.5	0.47	1.89
USA	2.82	11.26	33	3.75	14.98

Source: Research by Kurt Salmon Associates reported in *Apparel International* (1984), February.

Nor does the question of labour shortage take account of locational and ethnic divisions within the industry. If large primary-sector firms in predominantly white areas or areas of low unemployment (e.g. London) have difficulties in recruiting labour into an industry with long hours and low wages, small inner-city sweatshops drawing on ethnic-minority labour (whose employment alternatives are limited) experience few such difficulties. To the contrary, as we shall see, there is in fact a clothing-industry reserve army of minority women in areas such as the West Midlands. As Leigh and North put it succinctly: 'limited mobility and limited opportunities for alternative work (especially for Asian women) have created spatially and culturally confined labour markets in inner-city areas of the West Midlands' (Leigh and North, 1983: 43). Nor should it be assumed that the lack of labour shortages in this sector is related to the fact that the product requires a less skilled worker than the bigger plants that operate with more Taylorised production methods. Quite the reverse as Leigh and North emphasise:

Essentially this part of the sector remains a craft industry, and the labour process demands a good deal more skill from employees (especially from machinists who may be required to make through a complete garment) than in the mechanised volume producers.

(ibid.: 42)

What we are saying, therefore, is wages are low throughout the industry, deterring certain categories of workers, e.g. young white women, from entering the industry. Nevertheless, labour shortages where they do occur because of low pay and long hours have not been sufficiently problematic for firms to invest in labour-saving technology. As we shall see, labour savings are not the major consideration of firms who have invested in such technology.

There is, of course, yet another conventional wisdom in the industry that holds that rapid changes in fashion militate against investment in new technology. But as we shall see, one firm in particular operating in this sector chose technical innovation as the primary means of maintaining profitability at exactly the same time as many more traditional firms were going under (this firm is referred to as the 'innovator' in what follows). The firm's decision, taken in the late 1970s, to invest in new technology was motivated, it was argued by the financial director, by one factor: 'the need to respond quickly to changes in demand in the fast moving fashion business' ('Fashioned by Computer', *Financial Times*, 14 February 1984), thus flying directly in the face of conventional wisdom. The new micro-electronically related innovations in manufacturing equipment differ from their predecessors in being suited to, as well as reducing, the cost disadvantages of short runs and frequent changes in style.

Thus, ten years on, the British Apparel Association argues that all the primary-sector firms in the industry have largely followed suit, investing in labour-saving new technology backed up by the introduction of more flexible working practices. It needs to be re-emphasised that such firms constitute only a minority of producers in the sector. What exactly this technology is, how it has changed the labour process, and what its implications for employment in the industry are, will now be considered.

New technology, gender, and skill

The particular firm on which the description in this section is based is located in Yorkshire, employing 2,400 people on 20 sites in 1984. All design and cutting is centralised and none of the firm's production is subcontracted. As the downturn and unpredictability in consumer spending on clothing hit the industry in the late 1970s, the company moved up-market in style and price (at the time it was solely supplying to Marks and Spencer) and invested heavily in new technology. In order to grasp the changes in production brought about by the introduction of new technology (NT) we need to examine first the production process that preceded it. This brief discussion of the principal features of the production process relies heavily on the original Hoffman and Rush report on technical change in the clothing industry (Hoffman and Rush, 1983), Cynthia Cockburn's *Machinery of Dominance* (1985), and my own observations of the labour process in traditional and innovatory firms.

The pre-assembly processes involved are design, pattern-making, grading, and marker-making. Prior to the introduction of computer-aided design these pre-assembly operations consist of the following stages.

The designer produces a design for which she/he then makes up a rough pattern. A skilled pattern maker turns this into a workable pattern by the following methods. Master patterns (or blocks) are stored in the pattern room and represent standardised shapes for many different types of garments that are then adapted by the pattern maker to faithfully reflect the new design. The job of pattern maker is a highly skilled one requiring both designing and technical skills.

From this pattern, production engineers work out the various stages and costs of producing the garment. Most of these decisions and costings will be based on previous time-and-motion studies carried out by the firm on other styles. Hoffman and Rush argue that there are two main objectives being pursued at this stage: (1) with cloth accounting for up to 50 per cent of total costs the engineer must endeavour to minimise total fabric use; (2) when the assembly stage accounts for 80 per cent of labour costs, the engineer will also want to minimise the number of operations needed to assemble the garment (Hoffman and Rush, 1983, Section 3. 3).

The next step in this pre-assembly stage of production is called grading or sizing. Each pattern must be produced in different sizes – 10, 12, 14 etc., but these sizes also reflect rather different shapes so that a size 14 is not just a larger version of a size 10. The grading of patterns is therefore another skilled job requiring years of experience in order to obtain the right expertise and like pattern-making itself is 'as much an art as it is a science' (Hoffman and Rush, 1983, Section 3.5). The end product of the grading process is a nest of patterns.

Once the pattern has been graded, the most economical way in which to lay out the pieces of pattern on the cloth for cutting has to be decided. This is called lay-making and involves the creation of a paper marker indicating the optimum lay of the pattern on the cloth. Marker-making is another skilled job.

The cloth to be used for the production run then has to be inspected for flaws before it is spread from a roller in layers. The roller moves up and down the table with operators following the equipment to ensure an even lay of material. The number of layers spread on the cutting table will depend upon the size of the production run and the type of material to be used. The paper marker is then placed on top of the layers and cutting can proceed.

The cutting equipment is usually a hand-held, power driven reciprocating blade. Cutting is regarded as the most highly skilled task in the clothing labour process and as such has been monopolised by men. The cut pieces are then bundled and tagged and transported to the sewing room.

How the production process has changed with the introduction of NT, why it was adopted, and what it means for men's and women's jobs in the industry is considered below.

New tech, no sweat

Summing up the meaning of innovations in the pre-assembly stage, H. Joseph Gerber, President of Gerber Scientific Inc., put it this way:

> For many operations we can already take the human skills acquired over time by those directly involved in producing garments and translate them into instruction sets which direct a computer controlled machine to perform the same function as a skilled operator. The skill is thus memorised, transferable and can be replicated indefinitely.
>
> (Gerber, 1983: 90)

In short, micro-processor controlled equipment is deskilling and labour displacing; it robs the craftsperson of his or her skills and having memorised them applies them more accurately and efficiently than was ever previously possible.

In such a way, pattern-making has been revolutionalised through the introduction of computerised pattern-development systems. Basically, the standardised shapes represented by the master blocks have been digitised and can be displayed graphically by computer. When a new design arrives, instead of getting the cardboard blocks out for a particular garment type, the pattern technician (as she is now called) taps in the style number to the computer terminal and the block appears. With a stylus pen she points to the parts she wants and makes the necessary adjustments on screen to modify the master block to suit the new design requirements (Cockburn, 1985: 56).

The house rules governing grading are also 'digitised'. What this means is that the craft knowledge of the grader is converted into computer language and stored. The operator will also feed into the computer program information regarding measurement changes on each size. The computer now has all the information it needs to generate a graded nest of patterns that can be printed out as paper patterns, or onto card, or simply stored.

The next stage of pre-assembly operations – marker-making – combines the skill of the operator with the precise calculating capacity of the computer. The graded pieces of the pattern are displayed on the screen and using the stylus pen, the operator moves the pieces around until she finds what she knows from experience to be the best marker. The computer then takes over, calculating which pieces can be moved even closer, thus optimising fabric utilisation. The resultant best lay can then be plotted out and a magnetic tape can be produced that will guide computer-controlled cutters.

The job of cutter has been largely displaced, the task now mainly consisting of the insertion of a magnetic tape, checking that the material that has been spread automatically by spreading machines is accurate, and positioning the knife. The latter, driven by a numerically controlled motor and guided by the magnetic tape, can cut up to 300 layers of cloth at a time. For our key innovating firm, this not only means doubling output but reducing a job that used to take four cutters 3 hours to 8 minutes (Cockburn, 1985: 60; information supplied directly by the company).

Who benefits?

If firms are asked why they invest in new technology, labour-cost savings are not necessarily given primacy.

Of the 22 firms visited or who supplied detailed information for this study, 12 were manufacturers with their own production facilities. Only 3 had already invested and installed CAD and computer-aided cutting equipment (another had installed a system that was not yet in operation). When asked to list the benefits of this equipment, all 3 stated that it had enhanced productivity and efficiency. Other benefits listed were increased control over labour.

The two largest case-study firms (one with 4,820 employees spread over 20 plants and the other 2,400, also spread over 20 plants) had centralised design and cutting and subcontracted none of their production. The workers were members of the National Union of Tailors and Garment Workers, both were major suppliers to Marks and Spencer and emphasised the need to respond rapidly to fashion as their prime motivation for investment in new technology. This rationale flies in the face of received wisdom, which holds that it is rapid changes in fashion that militate against investment in new technology. But this is precisely where the new micro-electronically based innovations in manufacturing equipment are different from their predecessors in being suited to short runs and frequent changes in style. Using computer-aided design, one of the firms produces up to 200 new sample designs a week for its customers to choose from with any one in full production within two weeks of an order being placed. Computer-aided design is suited, in fact, to firms where a large number of short runs predominate.

Nevertheless, the introduction of micro-electronic innovations in the production of clothing is not in the view of the manufacturers guided solely by the imperative of increasing labour productivity and producing better quality products. Their diffusion should also be seen within the context of a continuing trend in the labour process that has been characterised by the subdivision of tasks and the de-skilling of labour with the possibility of enhanced control by management. Kaplinsky quotes from *Iron Age,* the journal of the American mechanical engineers, to illustrate this:

> Numerical control is more than a means of controlling a
> machine. It is a system, a method of manufacturing. It embodies
> much of what the father of scientific management, Frederick

Winslow Taylor, sought back in 1880 when he began his investigations into the art of cutting metal. 'Our original objective', Mr Taylor wrote, 'was that of taking control of the machine shop out of the hands of the many workmen and placing it completely in the hands of management'.

(*Iron Age*, 30 August 1976: 156 quoted in Kaplinsky 1984: 136)

Undoubtedly, the deskilling and displacement of all but a handful of highly skilled workers will continue.

Men and women: who benefits?

In her *Machinery of Dominance: Women, Men and Technical Know-How*, Cynthia Cockburn argues that: 'During the last half-century the industry has been undergoing a sex change. A slow but perceptible surge of women, entering by the sewing-room door, has been seeping across the cutting room and is now washing into pattern-room jobs' (Cockburn, 1985: 68).

Cockburn contends that the routinisation and fragmentation of cutting-room processes had already led to women 'seeping' into the cutting room and, simultaneously, women trained in design at college by dint of their over supply 'washing up' into pattern rooms. What this means, she goes on, is that during this period of transition from old to new technology, sex-typing of jobs is in confusion, firms using CAD having introduced single-sex departments or teams. She argues that it is in employers' interests to maintain segregation in order to evade equal pay legislation and as women have entered cutting-room jobs, relative earnings have slipped. In addition, the substitution of women for men makes sense given the fact that women come to the clothing labour process with certain skills in sewing, cutting, and the 'the diligence and niftiness that makes for a good keyboard or scope operator' (Cockburn, 1985: 71). Women do not possess these skills inherently, but the acquisition of such skills is a normal part of girls' socialisation – few boys are expected to learn or demonstrate such skills. Cockburn also argues that while women may stick at their jobs longer nowadays, employers will also benefit from young women leaving before they climb up off trainee rates of pay. The fact that the clothing industry can continue to insist on full-time hours and make no allowances for women's dual role in production as workers and mothers is bolstered by high levels of unemployment.

What, therefore, are the benefits if any for the workers? First, the personnel manager in our innovatory case-study firm confirmed that the introduction of NT was both deskilling and labour-displacing, but employment in the firm had increased overall as new orders out-stripped productivity improvements.

Second, the skill equation is as we have seen saturated with gendered constructions. Cynthia Cockburn argues:

> skilling and de-skilling is a subjective matter and the way each is
> experienced depends in part on the sex of the person in
> question. If some women would say they had gained a skill and
> many men would say they had been robbed of one, that would
> not be surprising. They have come from different places.
>
> (Cockburn, 1985: 65)

She maintains that the old skills (men's) were over-rated and myth-ologised, used not just by trade unions in the struggle against capital but as a 'male stratagem in the relative depreciation of women and women's work' (1985: 65).

Nevertheless, while new technology has brought women into operator roles, it has not, as Cockburn points out, brought them technical training or competence. Without that, women's new roles are highly vulnerable. What we are witnessing is part of an ongoing process, women being drawn into new roles in the labour process at one moment in a continuing trend towards further automation. The jobs of systems analyst, of senior manager, etc. are jobs that continue to be monopolised by men. The personnel director of the same firm saw the skill equation this way: 'When you introduce new technology you need a few extra specialists – but you take away the skills from a lot more' (*Financial Times,* 14 February 1984).

An ethnic division of labour?

If women are gaining jobs at the expense of men, however ambiguous that gain may be, who are those women? The answer to that question rests largely in geographical location. All the manufacturers visited, or who provided information in London, had a multi-ethnic work-force. Although CAD had been introduced into 2 firms in London (and was already in use in one of them) it was not possible to gain any information on whether and how new technology was changing the ethnic division of labour. Outside of London the location of many primary-sector firms does not coincide with areas of ethnic-minority residential concentration. Where it did, the firm reported an increase in the number of Asian women in the workforce but did not specify where in the production process those women had been assimilated.

Ethnic-minority women are heavily concentrated in secondary-sector firms with their low capital-to-labour ratios, the cost of CAD/CAM systems well beyond their reach. If such firms are to reap the benefits of new technology, then they require large injections of cash and technical assistance. Several local authorities have invested in new technology for collective use by small producers who are expected to comply with a code of conduct relating to employment practices as a condition of use. In this way, it is hoped that workers will share in the benefits accruing from the firms' access to NT. The experience has not always been good. Such a venture in Hackney, London was abandoned in 1986 amidst councillors' complaints about the Fashion Centre's commitment to monitoring of employment practices in firms using its services.

So far we have considered the technical changes in the pre-assembly stage of production. The fact that higher paid men monopolised these jobs in the past is not merely coincidental with their being the principal focus for the introduction of automation technologies.

Nevertheless, the assembly stage constitutes 30–40 per cent of total production costs and reducing the time spent handling as opposed to sewing the material has now become the focus for further automation research.

The assembly process

The EEC's Basic Research in Industrial Technologies for Europe (BRITE) programme is supporting 13 clothing projects. Courtaulds is a joint funder in one of these projects whose aim is to develop:

> a flexible manufacturing system for automated assembly for apparel from flexible materials. The objective of this project is to develop a system to take parts from the cutting room in ordered form, and using specially developed robotic handling systems, to carry out as much of the assembly and sewing process as possible in a 2-dimensional model ... it is estimated that in the bulk of production an average of 60 per cent of

operations can be carried out in this manner.

(Totterdill, 1988: 3)

To date the application of micro-electronics at the assembly stage has occurred in two principal ways, the first has been the development of dedicated equipment for high-volume, repetitive operations. Research carried out in Germany indicates that such equipment has limited flexibility (Weisbach, 1984).

The other development has been in the area of operator–programmable sewing machines. Such machines are general-purpose machines that the operator 'instructs' through a record-playback mechanism. One machine of this type observed during fieldwork was used to stitch collars. The operator reported that while the job had become more boring since the introduction of the electronic attachment, she enjoyed 'working this' (tapping the control box). The advantages for manufacturers are that such attachments are infinitely more flexible than their dedicated predecessors, changes requiring only a modification in the instructions programmed by the operator herself.

Nevertheless, the key to enhanced flexibility in the assembly process currently remains in the learnt skills of the operator (not in technology *per se*). In the immediate post-war period, most firms that relocated outside London adopted Taylorised production methods incorporating sectionalised assembly methods. Operatives tended to be trained for a limited range of tasks that they were expected to perform at very high speeds. But this type of labour process was suited to the more standardised longer production runs that suited the price, rather than the design-sensitive market, that predominated until the 1980s. As we have seen, the market has subsequently changed and firms such as our innovator case-study firm expect their machinists to become proficient in a much wider range of tasks. This is commonly referred to as multiskilling. In fact employees must sign an agreement on labour flexibility, which means that they may be called upon to do any job in the factory. Our case-study firm has gone some way to compensating machinists for the much lower levels of output such a labour process entails by paying their machinists higher basic rates of pay.

New technology in the office

There is little doubt that while many clothing producers in fashion-wear remain sceptical of the benefits of NT in the production process, most acknowledge its importance in the office. While none of the very small contractors visited during the course of this research had invested in office computers, others that were growing fast used them for accounting purposes, invoicing, and wages. In addition, as we have already noted, CAD enables producers to cost production more accurately and to maximise fabric utilisation. Also, Zeitlin and Totterdill argue that 'periodic reviews of factory performance are giving way to "real time" systems which monitor work-in-progress and assist managers in production planning, line balancing and work measurement' (Zeitlin and Totterdill, 1988: 21). They argue that as these systems of management information and production control become cheaper, they should be extremely attractive to small producers where management is usually overstretched and in many cases often involved in the production process itself.

New technology in fashionwear production: who benefits?

Contrary to popular belief, the production implications of a changed market in fashionwear demanding shorter runs of more highly differentiated fashion clothes should encourage producers to invest in new technology. The new micro-electronically based innovations are different from their predecessors in being suited to, as well as reducing the cost disadvantages of, short runs and frequent changes in style.

A Greater London Council Economic Policy Document (GLC Economic Policy Group, 1985: Appendix 1) summarises the changes in production technology as follows:

1. production control and stock control systems make it easier to handle a large number of short runs of garments;
2. computer-aiding, or complete automation of the pre-sewing stages of production are of greater benefit to shorter run production than to long, even though there are funding problems for many firms in acquiring this equipment;
3. some forms of improvement and computer-aiding of sewing machines are particularly appropriate for short batch production;

4. shorter runs tend to require greater machining skills.

(GLC Economic Policy Group, 1985: Appendix 1)

In theory, such changes should benefit the thousands of small firms that predominate in fashionwear production given their existing capacity for flexibility and the multiskilling of their workforces, particularly the ability of many machinists in this sector to make through a garment. But as we shall see in the next chapter, new technology is bypassing these firms, many of whom exist on very low profit margins due to the subcontracting stranglehold.

There is little doubt that as long as people want very cheap but fashionable clothes the secondary sector will continue to exist. But the more technically advanced sector outside London whose flexibility and speed is now greatly enhanced will undoubtedly increase competitive pressures on the secondary sector, which ultimately gets passed on to the already under-rewarded workforce in this sector through intensified work and further casualised working practices.

The duality in industrial structure of the contemporary fashionwear industry has been stressed. Some might argue that this duality reflects the development in Britain of a dual economy consisting of labour-intensive, low-wage industries alongside a high-wage, capital-intensive sector. The flaw in this argument is that the predominantly female workforce in the relatively capital-intensive sector of fashionwear production are not high earners, precisely because they are women. Nevertheless, all the primary-sector firms paid at least the minimum wage and observed the health and safety and statutory employment rights of their workers. It is precisely these guarantees of minimum wages and conditions that firms enmeshed in the lower strands of the subcontracting web flout.

Chapter five

The subcontracting web

Who benefits?

In Chapter 3 we argued that from the late 1960s onwards a combined strategy of technological gradualism and a continuing search for cheap labour was pursued by producers in Britain and the FRG in an attempt to restore international competitiveness. In both countries cheaper labour was found through subcontracting production, which in Britain has been the traditional method of reducing production costs and risks in the manufacture of clothing. In the FRG manufacturers began to exploit the labour-cost advantages of the new international division of labour by subcontracting work externally to low-wage countries and by importing a high proportion of fashion goods from Italy.

The drastic restructuring of the clothing industry as a whole, which accelerated after 1979, left the industry with a slim band of primary-sector firms in fashionwear, most of whom are now rapidly investing in the new flexible manufacturing technologies and who are favoured as producers by the newer design- and quality-conscious chains of fashion retailers. Most of these firms are not located in the inner cities where Britain's post-war black immigrants have settled.

In this chapter we turn our attention to the revitalisation and growth of a secondary sector of subcontractors producing fashion clothes in British inner cities. The coincidence of recession, high levels of unemployment, pockets of very cheap labour often based in the home, and an economic policy promoting unbridled free enterprise has led to a revitalised secondary sector, alongside and in some cases linked to the more technically advanced primary sector. While there is little doubt that this secondary sector has always existed, most commentators are agreed that its true size and recent rate of growth have gone largely unacknowledged at an official level (see

Euromonitor Report on the clothing industry (1985) for instance). Technological change has largely bypassed such firms, many of whom can compete with Third World producers not just on price but on other competitive factors such as speed of delivery and flexibility in production. Yet their competitive edge is often contingent upon their slipping in and out of the realms of legality and casualising low-paid labour. How the subcontracting web works is illustrated by a number of case studies. We will go on to consider critically the literature on ethnic entrepreneurship and to suggest an alternative theoretical formulation.

Fashionwear production in London

There is good evidence to suggest that those retailers targeting the fashion-orientated, over-25-year-old market are generally concentrating their production in factories outside London (Zeitlin and Totterdill, 1988). These retailers look directly to innovatory firms, such as our case-study firm in Chapter 4, who can combine speed, quality, and an in-house design output (GLC, Economic Policy Group, 1985).

Research carried out for this book indicated that there was less emphasis on technical change as a preferred strategy to maintain profitability amongst London firms. The long-standing 'tried and tested' system of subcontracting was regarded as preferable by most and for many small firms visited there was little choice.

A number of different types of clothing firm operate in London (though they all had one thing in common – the proprietors or senior managers were all men). The first type (and this is a very small group indeed – we found only 25 women's fashionwear firms left in London with more than 50 employees) produces up-market women's fashionwear (as one manager put it 'the kind of thing you splash out on for that special occasion'). The perceived main source of competition to the product of these firms was the Federal Republic of Germany. Three firms (operating out of 9 plants in London and one in Southeast Asia) fall into this category amongst the firms visited. Two of these firms had just invested in CAD, one in computer-aided cutting as well. The smaller of the firms employed 210 people with an output of 3,500 dresses per week, all of which were produced internally (they did not subcontract any of their production), while the larger, employing 1,600 people (and with an annual turnover of

£40m a year), subcontracted 10 per cent of its weekly output within London and another 10 per cent to Southeast Asia. The third firm subcontracted 33 per cent of its weekly output to 28 contractor firms in London (one of which we will take as a case study). On being questioned, one of the managers in the latter firm suggested that with an increasingly ageing workforce the firm would be pushed into a dual strategy of investment in computer-aided pre-assembly equipment combined with a more vigorous use of subcontractors for assembly processes. All of these firms are unionised and pay above the minimum wage (for example, £73 per week for a trainee finisher, January 1985). All complained of the lack of skilled labour, the loss of skilled machinists to other firms in London who paid 'clear money' (i.e. no deductions), and the difficulty of inducing youngsters into a low-pay industry in the capital where alternative sources of work were plentiful. All three firms are independent public companies, two of which grew out of long-standing Jewish family businesses. Jewish families have monopolised fashionwear production in London for well over a hundred years and still maintain a strong position as manufacturers, though their pre-eminence is now challenged by Greek-Cypriots. But just as Waldinger notes for New York: 'most are long-established firms, run by ageing owners whose children have chosen other pursuits. Consequently ethnic succession has created a space for new immigrant owners whose investment calculus is shaped by a very different assessment of the available opportunities' (Waldinger, 1986: 191). Several workers compared Jewish employers favourably with the more recent immigrant entrepreneurs, such as the Greek and Turkish Cypriots, Indian, Pakistani, and Bangladeshi employers. At an objective level, wages and conditions may be worse in the more recently established firms but this needs to be examined within the context of the position of these firms in the subcontracting hierarchy and the unbridled competition that exists in the sector as a whole.

The second group of firms (3) were also manufacturers but were involved in producing far more price-competitive garments for low-priced retail chains, supermarkets, and mail order firms (for instance C&A, Littlewoods, Woolworths, Tesco, and Asda). Two of the firms were heavily involved in subcontracting, one with 66 per cent of its production going to 44 outside contractors, another subcontracted 50 per cent of its production to CMT firms, and the third subcontracted variable amounts to 8 CMT firms depending on the time of year and the number of rush orders to be filled. The latter firm had invested heavily in new office and manufacturing equipment and saw this merely as a start to an ongoing programme of investment in new technology, though regarded investment in CAD/CAM systems to be well outside of its financial reach. In the past the same firm had subcontracted work to Cyprus due to what the managing director (himself Greek Cypriot) claimed were shortages of skilled machinists. He maintained that this, however, was no longer a problem due to liaison with schools and the establishment of the Youth Training Scheme. All three firms paid their in-house workers at least the agreed minimum rates with holiday pay. Again the employers complained of losing good workers to the clear-money sector.

Most commentators would probably argue that the final group of firms in the sample is more representative of London firms generally. In so far as the industry is bottom-heavy this is correct. This final group of firms consists of manufacturers who may have no production facilities of their own or maintain a purely skeleton staff for finishing garments as well as the great mass of subcontractors (8 of which were visited in London). The 4 'manufacturers' in this group were very varied. One had an output of 50,000 garments a week produced by 22 CMT firms throughout London, another producing 25,000 garments a week subcontracted 85 per cent of production to CMT firms in London and the rest abroad, having travelled widely to find the most suitable factories involved in outward processing. The other two manufacturers were small, production limited to 2,000–3,000 garments a week, in one case produced exclusively by homeworkers. While three of these firms were selling to the low-cost, high-fashion end of the market, one produced more up-market clothes, some under its own label.

The other firms in the group (8) are CMT firms, all of which exist in a highly precarious subcontractual position. All were owned by ethnic-minority entrepreneurs, some with ethnically homogeneous workforces. The majority were producing high-fashion, medium-to-poor-quality garments for the under-25 age group. Work in such firms tends to be highly erratic. Between September and December there is a full order book, overtime is plentiful, and homeworkers are employed to produce the excess.

As we have seen, the clothing industry has historically provided self-employment and work for immigrants in London and this pattern shows no signs of decline. More established immigrants subcontract to newer immigrants who in turn pass on the work and the risks to the most recently arrived. The competition is unregulated and cut-throat and price rather than quality is the main production criteria for the under-25, high-fashion market that it caters for. Currently, small firms in London are being squeezed on two sides. On one side from the more technically advanced sector outside of London whose speed and flexibility is now greatly enhanced, and on the other from contractors in the West Midlands who can undercut the already low wages that predominate in this sector in London. While it is very difficult to gauge exact wage differences from our interviews with factory workers (for instance in London, March 1985 we interviewed Bangladeshi male, factory-based machinists earning as little as £50 a week as well as Greek Cypriot female overlockers and machinists earning £130 or more), with homeworkers we were able to compare garments of similar style and complexity in terms of assembly and the prices that were paid for making them up in the two locations. Consistently, homeworkers received less per garment in the West Midlands compared to London (we examine the position of homeworkers in some detail in the next chapter). One manufacturer suggested to us that as a rule of thumb, a garment with labour costs totalling £2 in London could be made for as much as 50p less in the West Midlands. My own sense of the situation that existed in early 1985 was that while wages overall were lower in the West Midlands, Bangladeshi immigrant workers (the most recent excepting the Vietnamese of the post-war immigrants to gain a foothold in the London clothing industry) were earning the least of any workers in the London clothing industry and any discussion of ethnic entrepreneurship and labour must take the ethnic hierarchy that exists into account.

How the subcontracting chain works is best illustrated by a number of case studies, starting at the top end of the market.

Shifting the risks

Firm A is likely to have been one of the firms visited by Margaret Wray in her study of womenswear production in Britain in the 1950s. Originally a Jewish-owned producer of women's tailored outerwear in London, the firm moved out of London to South Wales during the Second World War. The firm has always produced fashionable and high-quality womenswear and continues to do so, though its range now goes beyond tailored outerwear to include less structured fashionwear. It has its own shops as well as 'shops-within-shops'.

The firm, now part of one of the largest independent clothing groups in the UK, had, in 1985, just undertaken an extensive re-equiping programme, installing state-of-the-art equipment at all stages of production with some government aid. Rather than use this high-capacity plant (fully unionised) for its own brand-name range it subcontracted a high proportion of the latter to Cut-Make-and-Trim firms, while using the South Wales plant to produce for Marks and Spencer.

One of the Cut-Make-and-Trim firms located in London was visited. The firm employed 28 full-time and 2 part-time workers on the premises in London's East End and another 12 homeworkers in the locality. The production was split 70 per cent on site and the rest produced by the homeworkers resulting in a weekly turnover of £10,000–£12,000. All the homeworkers had previously worked on site and were fully skilled in all aspects of assembly.

The production process was based on traditional methods with men carrying out lay-making and cutting processes. There was also one black male machinist. The workforce was unionised; machinists' pay (early 1985) varied between £98 and £140 a week.

The proprietor (Jewish) explained that cost was not the only deterrent to investment in new technology. More importantly in his view were the obstacles to his breaking into manufacturing with regular contracts from the chain retailers, which he believed was vital if such investment were to be made. In addition, he saw the introduction of CAD by manufacturers and computer-aided cutting reducing the profit he made from 'cabbage'. The latter is the cloth left over after cutting an order. As the manufacturer who places the order pays for or supplies the cloth, then any surplus after cutting can be profitably used by the contractor to make up additional garments and many contractors claim that this is where their profit margins rest. If the manufacturer who places the order invests in CAD and/or computer-aided cutting, both of which eliminate waste in fabric utilisation, then the contractor's cabbage goes with it.

Firm B is a 'manufacturer' that deals directly with retailers as well as wholesalers in the fashionwear industry. It has an output of 25,000 dresses, skirts, separates etc. per week, output steadily increasing in the preceding 5-year period. Eighty-five per cent of output is produced by subcontractors in the UK, 10 per cent is outward processed in 6 factories abroad, and only 5 per cent of weekly output is actually manufactured by the firm itself. Design is centralised and the most up-to-date knitting and embroidery machines are used in the firm's own plant to ensure a distinctive look is maintained in the finished product. Fifty per cent of output is exported and the firm had received a Queen's Award for Export Achievement.

Firm C is a very different kind of operation – a small-scale producer who had broken straight into manufacturing and export. Mr X had been made redundant from a plastics factory six months prior to the interview. Redundancy money was used to buy an Eastman cutter, textiles, wood for making tables, and to pay rent for very small premises. Through a relative he made contact with an agent exporting dresses to Saudi Arabia and they made a deal for a small test contract at a very competitive price. He and his brother (the latter had worked in the fashionwear industry since migrating from Pakistan) marked up and cut the cloth for very simply styled women's and girls' dresses. These were put in his van and delivered to between 12 and 20 homeworkers (depending on the size of the order), all Asian women, known personally to himself and his wife. The sewn garments were picked up, brought back, and trimmed and finished by his wife. If there was no work there were no employees to be retained.

Firm D is a Turkish Cypriot CMT firm that produces cheap high-fashion clothes for one of the high street chains targeting the under-25 age group. Mr D does not deal with them directly; he always works through a manufacturer without production facilities of his own. Only 6 workers including his mother and sister work on the premises where all cutting, trimming, and finishing is carried out. The bulk of assembly work is carried out by a fluctuating labour force of homeworkers who produce up to 2,000 garments a week.

Firm E, also a Turkish Cypriot CMT firm, operated on a very similar basis. Around 50 per cent of the assembly work was completed on the premises by 7 machinists and the rest by a fluctuating workforce of homeworkers. Mr D produced clothes for one retailer only (again their relationship mediated by a manufacturer) which, he argued, 'was in trouble with its image'. Like many others interviewed he said he would shift more work to homeworkers if he could find more with factory-learnt skills.

Retailers' mark-up on ex-factory prices varies between 70 and 130 per cent, though some contractors argued it could be as high as 200 per cent. The subcontracting web is a hierarchy with each descending layer getting squeezed a little harder. For the contractors it is, as one trade unionist put it, a 'dog-eat-dog' situation, their survival dependent upon an under-rewarded and often casualised workforce. Officially 43 per cent of the 60,000-strong clothing workforce in London is composed of ethnic minorities, but this 1979 Labour Force figure would not take proper account of illegal immigrants or homeworkers (Morokvasic *et al.*, 1986: 411).

In a *Report on the Clothing Industry and Public Sector Investment in East London*, the National Union of Tailors and Garment Workers and the Hackney Trade Union Support Group argue:

> The employers operate in a ruthlessly competitive market ... trying to make a living in a very insecure industry. They mainly do outwork for larger firms. Operations like design, marketing, forward planning, skill training just do not exist in these firms. The employers operate under very tight margins and once they fail to fulfil an order, at the price and in the time, demanded by the manufacturer they will lose future orders from that manufacturer. Many of the employers are quite ruthless, they operate on the backs of their workers ... they employ direct a small number of workers (often so-called 'self-employed' or 'off the book'), they do not deduct the proper tax and national insurance, they do not pay overtime or holiday pay, they do not abide by the employment and health and safety at work legislation. All these practices keep the employers' overheads to a minimum. The firms are in fact producing fashion garments for the major fashion multiples like British Home Stores, Chelsea Girl, and Richard Shops. They are part of a long chain of companies taking orders from large companies and then putting them out to manufacture by the small CMT firms that proliferate in the London clothing trade.
>
> (NUTGW, 1983: 6–7)

When a firm incurs large debts or wishes to avoid the scrutiny of the Inland Revenue Fraud Squad, liquidation of the company is not an uncommon solution resorted to by the proprietors of these small firms. This does not of course exclude a rapid reappearance under a new trading name, with exactly the same workforce. In fact, workers have reported working for the same boss under five different company names (Anthias, 1983; NUTGW and Hackney Trade Union Support Group, 1983; Bishton, 1984). It is within this context that we need to consider with some scepticism the reported high rate of company failures in this sector (see, for instance, Department of Employment, 1976).

Fashionwear production in the West Midlands

In the West Midlands a whole 'new' clothing industry has taken off on this basis largely since 1978. Asian male workers were recruited throughout the 1960s to work in West Midlands metal-manufacturing and engineering industries. Yet between 1975 and 1982, 74 per cent of all industrial job losses in the area were in those industries and in areas of Asian residential concentration, unemployment rates had risen to between 40 and 47 per cent (Gaffikin and Nickson, n. d.)

With continuing high levels of racial discrimination in Britain (see Brown, 1984) entrepreneurship has become a necessity for many minority men shaken out of labour-intensive work. In many ways entrepreneurship can then be regarded as a form of disguised unemployment with earnings often much lower than those that prevailed during wage-labouring days (Aldrich *et al.*, 1984).

A small redundancy payment is enough to set oneself up as a clothing producer if there is also access to skilled, cheap, and flexible labour. Asian women have become the predominant suppliers of that labour in what has become the only manufacturing growth sector in the West Midlands economy. The West Midlands Low Pay Unit (WMLPU) survey carried out in 1984 reported that:

> There was a ready supply of local labour, particularly among Asian women, and again the workforce was at first composed of relatives or the same close contacts.... Expansion has meant wider recruitment, and some firms now advertise for machinists on local Asian radio programmes, and by posters and door-to-door leaflets.
>
> (West Midlands Low Pay Unit, 1984: 12)

It is estimated that at least 20,000 new jobs have been created in small clothing firms in the area since 1979 (West Midlands Low Pay Unit, 1984). Nevertheless both the WMLPU and Mitter argue that this may still underestimate the real size of the industry and the labour force because of unregistered firms and undeclared homeworkers. In 1988 researchers at the National Unit on Homeworking in Birmingham estimated that for every factory worker in the West Midlands clothing industry there are two unregistered homeworkers

(Rai and Sheikh, 1989, forthcoming). Mitter argues that a far larger number of workers would be needed than official figures suggest to maintain current levels of output in women's fashionwear nation-wide, a sector where, she contends, 'Significant changes in the aver-age productivity of labour are ... highly unlikely' (Mitter, 1986: 70). The discrepancy, she maintains, 'between the implied levels of em-ployment and registered levels could imply a transference of jobs (13,100) from the factory to the sweatshops and home-based sector' (ibid.: 70).

While the assertion that 'significant changes in productivity are highly unlikely' needs to be questioned given the type of technical change we have described as occurring in primary-sector firms, there is little doubt that for the vast majority of producers in fashionwear this statement is correct in so far as technical change is simply pas-sing them by.

Just like its London counterpart, there is no evidence to suggest that new technology is a feature of the new West Midlands industry, which caters primarily for the cheap, low-quality end of the market with well over half of the firms acting as CMT subcontractors in women's fashionwear. In 1984 the chairperson of the Asian Traders Association in the West Midlands estimated that 100,000 garments a week were moving between West Midlands CMT firms and Lon-don manufacturers (West Midlands Low Pay Unit, 1984: 13). The attraction, pointed out to me by several contractors in London, is the lower labour costs in the West Midlands. Even though the legal minimum wage set by the Clothing Wages Council is low relative to average national earnings (it is argued by the Council that the rate should be fixed at the level that the least efficient firm can afford, a dubious rationale given that the Wages Councils were set up to en-sure that *workers* in the industry got a living wage) workers in the new West Midlands clothing industry were being paid on average around £1 an hour in 1983 which was 50p an hour less than the legal minimum rate (WMLPU, 1984: 19).

But homeworkers are paid even less, sometimes as little as 15p a garment. Two questions about homeworking usually spring to mind: (1) How can employers get away with paying so little? and (2) surely homeworking is a very inefficient form of production? The answer to the first question is simply that there are not adequate policing mechanisms to enforce minimum pay and other aspects of employ-ment protection. Employers are meant to register homeworkers with the local authority, but in 1985 only 1 homeworker was listed on the register in Birmingham City Council and the Wages Inspectorate, which in theory can police the wages of homeworkers, has been cut by a third since 1979. The response to the second question is yes, homeworking is a very inefficient form of production, not just one person, one machine, but one person, one home. The difference is that that person owns her machine, pays her own rent, pays her own heating bills, has to shoulder all responsibility for sickness, being laid off, holidays, retirement, tax, and national insurance. The supplier of homework has got rid of all his responsibilities as an employer at a stroke. Mr X, whose operation we described above, explained that as long as the homeworkers live in the same neighbourhood, operating costs including his time and petrol can be kept to a minimum.

A systematic study of clothing firms in Coventry in 1987 indicates that (a) only 2 firms out of 66 in the city are non-Asian owned; (b) 95 per cent of the workforce is Asian; (c) start-up capital (usually under £5,000) was found either from personal or family sources; (d) only a minority of firms in the city were involved in complete manufacturing (27); (e) those that were, 'either supply the non-fashion end of the market where major design changes are infrequent or produce clothes, the design for which can easily be copied'; (f) only one firm in the city was unionised and only 15 of the firms employed more than 25 people (Healey *et al.*, 1988).

What we have witnessed, therefore, is the rise of what appears to be a largely dependent 'ethnic economy' in the sense that few of the firms established over the last 10 years have their own design or marketing capacity to lift them out of the subcontracting stranglehold. As the 1985 *Euromonitor Report* on the clothing industry concludes:

> a major factor fuelling growth in this sector was the emergence
> of major customers, including many famous High Street names
> who found in these small workshops a flexibility that matched
> the changing patterns of consumer demand they were
> experiencing. Existing manufacturers found it difficult to
> respond to these changes in the market, the new small firm
> sector with its low overheads, short production runs and ability
> to cope with rush orders filled this new found need.
>
> (*Euromonitor*, 1985: 47)

By late 1984, there was sufficient public concern over dangerous working conditions (five workers had been killed in a fire in a sweatshop in Mile End, East London in 1983) and the payment of illegally low wages (highlighted by the WMLPU Report and other evidence) for the Chairman of the Conservative Party (in government) to announce that a 'campaign against sweatshops' was being waged by the factory and wages inspectors (it should be pointed out that the Inspectorate had been cut by a third compared to 1979 manning levels so that a firm might expect a visit once in every 19 years) and local fire authorities in Leicester, the West Midlands, and the East End of London ('Gummer unveils offensive on sweat shops', the *Guardian,* 11 September 1984: 2). Mr Gummer suggested that a minority of 'bad bosses' were subjecting 'decent' employers to unfair competition. Six months later, Peter Bottomley, the Employment Under-Secretary reported that the official investigation found that much public alarm over dangerous working conditions and underpayment in sweatshops was unjustified. Alec Smith, General Secretary of the National Union of Tailors and Garment Workers responded 'If you believe that, you'll believe anything' and argued that the report had in fact revealed 'appalling' problems ('Fear unjustified over conditions in sweatshops', *Financial Times,* 28 February 1985: 5).

Being your own boss

The encouragement of small business generally has, of course, been a major plank of Thatcher government policy. In the wake of the 1981 Brixton disturbances, Lord Scarman's claim that black people had to secure a 'real stake in their community' through business enterprises lent further weight to the Conservative government's conviction that the front-line victims of deepening recession and de-industrialisation should pick themselves up by their ethnic boot-straps.

The publication of the third Policy Studies Institute study entitled *Black and White Britain* testified to the rise in self-employment among Asians in Britain compared to the 1974 survey. Ten years on, Asian men and women were more likely to be self-employed than white men and women, while Caribbean men and women remained under-represented within the ranks of the self-employed. Other surveys also indicate over-representation of Turkish and Greek Cypriot men (22 per cent) and Chinese amongst the ranks of the self-employed (Anthias, 1983; Baxter and Raw, 1988). Unfortunately, the term 'ethnic minorities' is defined narrowly by the Department

Table 5.1 The self-employed: ethnic minorities and whites compared

	white	ethnic minorities	West Indian	Indian	Pakistani/ Bangladeshi	Other non-white
Males	14.0	17.7	8.5	23.7	21.4	17.4
Fem	6.6	5.8	0.9	9.4		4.7

Source: Spring 1985, Labour Force Survey, *Employment Gazette,* January 1987: 22

of Employment's analysis of Labour Force Survey data and does not include the latter ethnic minorities. Table 5.1 represents the data for non-white self-employed compared to white.

Self-employment is often used as an indicator of entrepreneurship, but I would suggest that it is not a particularly good one. Many of the clothing workers who were interviewed during the course of this research were technically self-employed because their boss was not interested in shouldering the costs or responsibilities of being an employer. In reality, they receive work from only one company. Many are actually working on its premises and they are supervised. Thus they are expected to behave as employees without any of the benefits of employee status. The same applies to homeworkers who do not control the amount of work they are given, how it is to be done, or who they can sell it to. In all cases the employer has control over these factors (Roxby, 1984: 18). Examining the various legal tests used to ascertain employment status, Roxby concludes that the 'entrepreneurial' approach tested by the answer to the question 'Is this person her/his own boss?' ultimately proves to be the most significant of all the factors in deciding the nature of an employment relationship (Roxby, 1984: 29).

In short, using aggregate data on the self-employed as a basis for measuring the rate of entrepreneurship may be somewhat unreliable. Bearing this in mind one may still cautiously endorse the claim that some ethnic groups are over-represented in business and others under-represented when compared with the population generally (see Ward and Jenkins, 1984 for evidence on Britain). In the context of the fashionwear industry we are particularly interested in why it is that certain post-war ethnic groups such as the Greek and Turkish Cypriot, Indian, Pakistani, and Bangladeshi communities have become garment entrepreneurs and not other ethnic groups such as the Afro-Caribbean and Irish.

Paralleling government enthusiasm for small business, there is a growing academic interest and literature in Britain on ethnic entrepreneurship. Much of this literature is theoretically rooted in what has been termed the 'sociology of ethnic relations' (Phizacklea, 1984: 205). Such studies have been keen to move away from an emphasis on the migrant/immigrant as an object of racism, discrimination, and exploitation to the way in which ethnic ties can be used as a resource, for example, in creating alternative employment opportunities.

There is substantial evidence in the literature to suggest that: (1) ethnic business is predominantly labour-intensive; (2) access to family or community members as low-wage employees is a key competitive advantage for many ethnic entrepreneurs; and (3) there are differential rates of entrepreneurship between ethnic groups.

I want to suggest that these differential rates of entrepreneurship can be partly explained by differential rates of access to cheap and flexible female labour power. Extant theories of 'ethnic' entrepreneurship take little account of the impact that racial discrimination, harassment, and violence may have on the retention, even development, of so-called ethnic ties, solidarity, and social structure, including the retention of a clearly defined sexual division of labour and the confinement of women to 'safe' environments. If the mainstream avenues to lucrative employment are cut off by racism and discrimination, then the adaptation of available skills and resources within a particular group to alternative, income-generating mechanisms is a reasonably predictable outcome. Of vital importance to that strategy is the use of women's so-called natural skills and their labour as a resource. All the extant theories stress the importance of the family (real or fictive) based economy, yet they ignore the gender-specific mechanisms of subordination therein that generate a supply of low-wage or unpaid labour, ensuring the viability of the labour-intensive enterprise. When authors refer to 'the family' they are nearly always referring to women, for example:

> Labour costs can be kept down, where the time of family
> members is available to assist with the business and where,
> either through racism, economic factors or cultural
> prescriptions, there is little alternative to working in a firm run
> by a community member. A community where immigration is
> largely by males, or at least not in complete family units, as with

the Irish, is therefore at a disadvantage in this respect. Since
most ethnic business is labour intensive, access to family or
community members as employees at low rates is a key
advantage for many entrepreneurs.

(Mars and Ward, 1984: 18)

What I am suggesting is that ethnic business is predominantly male-
controlled and labour-intensive; men are bosses and women are predominantly workers. This is not unique to ethnic business in so far as
fewer women than men are entrepreneurs in the population as a
whole. In the early 1980s a study was carried out in Lambeth, London, comparing black with white businesses. The black sample, consisting of 33 Afro-Caribbean and 70 Asian businesses, were identi-
fied through a mailing to all firms in Lambeth followed up by con-
tacts with local-community representatives. A hundred white businesses of the same type and size were selected from the land-use reg-
istry. Only 10 per cent of all owners/managers in the sample were
women and this broke down as 15 per cent of the white firms and 5
per cent of Afro-Caribbean, but no Asian, firms had women
owner/managers (Brooks, 1982).

Set against this low level of entrepreneurship amongst women is
the fact that in many labour-intensive businesses women predominate as workers. My contention is that those ethnic groups deemed
to be more successful in the business world than others are characterised by social structures that give easier access to female labour
subordinated to patriarchal control mechanisms.

Patriarchy is used here in a materialist sense and in accordance
with both Cockburn and Hartmann's definition, who view patriarchy
as:

A set of social relations which has a material base and in which
there are hierarchical relations between men and solidarity
among them, which enables them in turn to dominate women.
The material base of patriarchy is men's control over women's
labour power. That control is maintained by excluding women
from access to necessary economically productive resources and
by restricting women's sexuality.

(Cockburn, 1985: 84, following Hartmann, 1979)

It is widely recognised in the literature that access to family or community members as low-wage workers is a key competitive advantage

for many ethnic businessmen. What is usually glossed over is the extent to which this family or community labour is female and subordinated to very similar patriarchal control mechanisms in the workplace as in the home. When such factors are recognised there is often slippage on the gender front. For instance, Mars and Ward argue that in the case of Turkish Cypriot clothing firms and restaurants:

> The 'captive' labour supply provided by immigrant wives, whose way of life keeps them largely separate from the wider society, is vital to the success of the enterprise, as is the interest of potential entrepreneurs in accepting low wages for their work in return for gaining the experience which will equip them to set up on their own in due course.
>
> (Mars and Ward, 1984: 4)

What they fail to distinguish is the fact that the fringe benefit of entrepreneurship is reserved for men and this is something that Clark and Rughani argue is developed and learnt within the male subculture and extended kin group (Clark and Rughani, 1983). Westwood (1988) and Tambs Lyche (1982) make the same point with regard to Gujerati men, suggesting that their masculinity is socially constructed in relation to enterprise, trade, profit, and abilities in the world of business. Sallie Westwood goes on to suggest that:

> Enterprises are often termed 'family businesses', invoking both a familial ideology and its practices in terms of commanding resources held within the family. In fact, the enterprises that mark Gujerati communities in Britain are clearly bound to men and male strategies in relation to the household, and women may have no part in the decision making surrounding business and commercial ventures although women take great pride in the family enterprises, referring to 'our shop' or 'our business' in ways that express their commitment.
>
> (Westwood, 1988: 121)

Likewise Sasha Josephides suggests that Greek Cypriot women working in cafés with their husbands see themselves building up a family business even though their husbands are registered as managing the business and the wife possibly only registered as his employee (Josephides, 1988: 43).

The use of wives and daughters as unpaid labour in the subcontracting firms visited during research for this book was common. In these circumstances women are working under patriarchal relations of production, remaining dependent for their maintenance on the 'boss' who is usually also the head of household in return for their efforts. As will be pointed out later, the sexism built into British immigration law (particularly after the passing of the 1962 Act, which allowed men to be joined by their wives and children but did not give women the same rights) not only reinforces this notion of 'family women' but also places severe constraints on the terms upon which they can enter British labour markets.

As Sallie Westwood amd Parminder Bhachu suggest:

> The fact that many minority women came as 'family women' or on vouchers acquired through the promise of a job in a relative's business has had a major impact on the way in which they have been integrated into the capitalist economy. They have not been 'free labourers' in the conventional sense and, therefore, part of an open labour market (which is an ideal that is often cross-cut by familial and social relations in all sectors). Family businesses have been able to access minority women's labour power through the mediations of kinship and an appeal to ideologies which emphasise the role of women in the home as wives and mothers and as keepers of family honour.
>
> (Westwood and Bhachu, 1988: 5)

As firms begin to expand, recruitment of labour will extend beyond the family but initially at least will remain within the same ethnic group (Hoel, 1982; Anthias, 1983; Waldinger, 1986). Anthias and Josephides both make the point that because of the many ties that Greek Cypriot employers have with their employees the relationship can never be seen simply in economic terms resulting in the women workers being highly exploited (Anthias, 1983; Josephides, 1988). Nevertheless, Josephides argues that women working for outside employers recognise that exploitation for what it is, 'though often they can do nothing about it' (Josephides, 1988: 49).

Similar conflicting pressures face Asian women in the West Midlands clothing industry. Yet with staggeringly high levels of unemployment for Asian men and women in the West Midlands, racism and exclusionary practices in other sectors of the labour market, and the claims of 'ethnic loyalty', workers are in a very weak position to resist such exploitation. The threat of unemployment and the knowledge that there are other minority women who can be substituted for the same job, act as a powerful deterrent to resistance amongst an already vulnerable workforce. Nevertheless, such pressures have not deterred Asian women from struggling for union recognition in their workplaces in a number of notable disputes in the region (for example, the Kewal Bros dispute in 1984). In most cases employers have won by using the tactic of closing down the firm and reopening under a new name with a completely different workforce (Bishton, 1984).

But these processes rest on the constraints imposed upon a generation of *immigrant* women, women who are determined that their daughters will not follow them into the low-pay ghettoes to which they have been confined.

What I am suggesting, therefore, is that familial ideologies have been usefully brought into play in ensuring the viability of a particular economic form, that is, labour-intensive business. But these ideologies must be understood within a context where family immigration or reunion has taken place within a framework of racist and sexist practices – practices that are built into the very fabric of immigration legislation.

Thus the pattern of family immigration or reunion is probably quite closely connected with the rate of business start-ups in labour-intensive industries such as clothing. For both Greek and Turkish Cypriot women, migration to Britain took a number of forms. If married, women came with their husbands or joined them usually not more than a year or two later. If unmarried, they often came to join married siblings or even to live with an employer, mainly in the clothing industry (Josephides, 1988; Ladbury, 1984). Asian and Chinese women coming mainly to Britain after 1962 to join husbands or fathers entered under more formal constraints. In their analysis of the ethnic fast-food industry, Baxter and Raw argue that in the case of Chinese women: 'Dependants, however, were obliged to demonstrate that they could be supported by their sponsors, which rendered them in a far more subordinate position than women who had emigrated independently from urban Hong Kong and Singapore' (Baxter and Raw, 1988: 65).

I would suggest that the situation has been very different for Afro-Caribbean migrants where the rate of independent female migration was high and the aspirations of women to gain financial independence and security through migration well documented (Phizacklea, 1982; Dex, 1983; Stone, 1983). As a result, Afro-Caribbean businesses are not characteristically labour-intensive (Ward and Reeves, 1984) in terms of start-up. Afro-Caribbeans are likely to opt for the partnership rather than the family-style approach to business and have less reliance on family or ethnic group labour than Asian businesses (Wilson and Stanworth, 1988). In addition most evidence points to a higher rate of female entrepreneurship amongst Afro-Caribbeans though, to reiterate, this is uniformly low across all ethnic groups (Wilson and Stanworth, 1985).

In addition, if we compare Britain with the Federal Republic of Germany where family reunion and self-employment have never been encouraged, we cannot find evidence of any ethnic entrepreneurship in the clothing industry, beyond the fur trade and repair shops (Morokvasic *et al.*, 1986). The same was true of the Netherlands until 1975 when the restrictions on family reunion were liberalised. Boissevain reports that this coincides with the re-emergence of a secondary sector of clothing production in Amsterdam.*

Explaining the differences

There is of course a wide range of existing theory that claims to explain why some ethnic groups are more widely represented within entrepreneurial ranks than others. 'Middleman minority' theories aim to analyse the position of groups distinguished by their concentration in independent trading and commercial activities, occupying a petit-bourgeois class position. A range of theories falls within this conceptualisation, some of which emphasise contextual factors. For instance, the argument that such groups are creations of the dominant class in a society, acting as a go-between for the ruling elite in their dealings with subordinate classes. This in turn generates a hostile reaction towards the middleman group (Blalock, 1967; and Hamilton, 1978).

A variant of this approach is argued by Pierre van den Berghe who maintains that any similarities that do exist among middleman minorities must be sought 'principally in the social structure of the plural society as a whole, and only secondarily in the characteristics of the immigrant groups' (van den Berghe, 1975: 198).

Edna Bonacich and John Modell argue that such contextual the-

---

* This point was made by Jeremy Boissevain at the 'Clothing Industry' workshop of the Ethnic Business Conference, Aston University Management Centre, Birmingham, May 1985.

ories are unsatisfactory if they assume that the minorities are the creation of the society in which they reside. They suggest that there is plenty of evidence to show that some groups and not others come to concentrate in the middleman category regardless of context. They list these as Jews, Chinese, and Indians (Bonacich and Modell, 1980: 31; and Appendix B).

Edna Bonacich in her earlier work propagated a view that the initial orientation of the group towards its territory will have a significant impact on the economic role it comes to play. Her view is that groups who see themselves as temporary migrants or 'sojourners' encourage their concentration in trade and similar middleman lines. They promote hard work, risk-taking, and concentration in liquidatable lines. Indirectly, they encourage the retention of ethnic solidarity, which aids ethnic business (Bonacich, 1973). In her later work with John Modell the concern is whether or not the ethnic ties dissolve once the viability and/or necessity of the economic form declines (Bonacich and Modell, 1980).

Some of the most widely propagated theories are cultural in form. Rather than viewing middleman groups as creatures of the society they come to or settle in, such theories concentrate on the characteristics they bring to this environment. For instance, Ivan Light (1972) argues that strong ascriptive ties enable some ethnic groups to succeed in entrepreneurial activity where the contractual relationships characteristic of industrialised societies may be less successful. Other theories are based on the belief that certain ethnic groups have an elective affinity with business. Such theories draw heavily on Weber's *The Protestant Ethic and the Spirit of Capitalism* (1958). Culturally valued attributes such as hard work and risk-taking are seen to be particularly well suited to entrepreneurial success.

Waldinger has argued that 'cultural' theories can be described as 'the entrepreneurial-values' approach and usefully split into a 'hard' and 'soft' form. The hard form ascribes these values to a belief system independent of a group's economic role, while the soft form would see entrepreneurial values as an adaptation to the original conditions in which a group lived (Waldinger, 1986: 7).

Waldinger's objections to both can be summarised as follows: as far as the hard form is concerned, if groups possess such characteristics, why is it over generations, sometimes just one, that they move from over-representation as entrepreneurs to an employment profile identical to the population as a whole? In addition, he argues that the conditions of the hard form are difficult to meet in so far as evidence would have to be found of business-relevant values that are not reducible to a group's pre-migration experiences (ibid.: 7). I would want to add that the hard form verges on a racist explanation because it implies that such traits are inherent.

Waldinger argues that both the hard and the soft form play down or ignore the fact that:

> the bundle of traits, attitudes and behavioural patterns that are 'cultural' are themselves the product of previous interaction between a group and its original environment; consequently, if these cultural patterns can be successfully transferred from one society to another, then it is likely that the two societies resemble one another in some important respects ... hence culture will influence an immigrant group's economic life to the extent that it is congruent with the new environment of the host society.

> (Waldinger, 1986: 9)

My own view is that retention of norms and practices such as those relating to appropriate gender roles may, in a climate of racism and economic decline, both be reinforced and literally 'put to work'. Such practices can then be used to underpin the viability of alternative income-generating mechanisms when the mainstream avenues to lucrative employment are cut off for both men and women by racism.

Finally, cultural explanations can easily fall into the stereotype trap and act as a self-fulfilling prophecy. The 'ethnic economy' provides employment for minority women confronted by continuing high levels of racism and racial discrimination and a reduction in traditional job opportunities in manufacturing industry (Phizacklea, 1987). But it is also argued that work in this sector is dictated by certain disadvantages that they carry around with them such as language deficiencies, cultural preferences, and lack of recognised skills, facets of what Morokvasic (1983) describes as a conventional stereotype of minority women. That stereotype can provide a useful justification for exploitation as the following quote from one Asian entrepreneur in Coventry illustrates:

> I see the majority of women working for me as benefiting from my job offer. They are illiterate and have no skills, hence no

British factory will make use of them. Their £20 a week will help towards the family income, and we are like a big family here.

(Hoel, 1982: 86)

In the next chapter we will show how this is a completely inaccurate picture of women's skills and the attitude they have to their work in an industry into which they have had little choice but to enter, given the high levels of racial and gender segregation in British labour markets.

Thus to sum up our discussion of entrepreneurship I want to suggest that, following Mars and Ward (1984) and Waldinger (1986), there are basically two conditions that are vital in ethnic entrepreneurship. One is access to resources that not all entrepreneurs can lay their hands on and I see a low-wage, flexible labour force as crucial in this respect. The other condition is to find an economic niche in which the small firm can viably function. I suggest that the conditions that to a large extent have always existed in the fashion-clothing production industry and have been intensified since the late 1970s make it a favoured niche for 'seed-bed' ethnic business.

Finally, it is imperative to recognise that it is racism and racial discrimination that constrain choice and force many minority men into the entrepreneurial option and thus minority women to work for them. In the clothing industry the only way in is usually at the bottom of a dog-eat-dog, subcontracting chain, which means up to 200 per cent mark-ups for retailers and paltry sums for subcontractors and their retinue of workers and homeworkers.

Chapter six

Working the seam
Minority women in fashionwear production

In this chapter, my concern is to examine the supply of labour to the small secondary-sector firms in the fashion-clothing industry. It is this labour supply, I have argued, that has formed the building blocks for such firms and without which they would not remain economically viable given the fierce competition that exists in the sector.

In order to understand the conditions which largely shape that labour supply, I need to examine the racist and sexist context that relegates minority women to a subordinate position in social relations prior to their entry into the labour market. These racist and sexist practices have been enshrined in British immigration legislation which reinforces and therefore aids the reproduction of patriarchal expectations of women's dependency on men. How these forces combine to subordinate minority women is most dramatically illustrated by their presence in the manufacturing, homeworking labour force.

All women workers in the clothing industry in Britain earn less than the manufacturing average for women workers for long hours (there is very little part-time work in the clothing industry) and a socially constructed notion of the skills that they bring to their work. Nevertheless, the impact of racism and ethnicity is clearly etched on the employment profiles of black and ethnic-minority women in the British clothing industry.

In Chapter 5 I emphasised how some ethnic entrepreneurs have been able to gain access to co-ethnic female labour through kinship links (real or fictive) and an appeal to familial ideologies. But as Swasti Mitter has argued: 'It would be unfair to attribute the rise of sweatshops and homeworking in these communities solely to the patriarchal values of Asians and Cypriots' (1986: 57).

The business strategies of ethnic-minority men must be understood within the context of constraints imposed upon their employment options by continuing high levels of racism and economic decline in Britain. Racism has also ensured that minority women are defined as the bearers of inferior labour prior to their entry into British labour markets. But sexist immigration legislation has reinforced and aided the reproduction of patriarchal expectations of women's dependency. For instance, the labour migrations from the Indian subcontinent were male-led; these men were 'target' workers, their expectation to return home with enough money to buy land, a business, etc. But the introduction of restrictive immigration legislation for Commonwealth citizens in 1962 changed all that. The possibility of never being able to return to Britain if they left prompted many men to encourage their wives and children to join them. I have suggested elsewhere that one might regard this as a kind of insurance policy against unforeseen mishaps (Phizacklea, 1983). Thus the fact that many minority women had little choice but to enter as family women or on a voucher sponsored by a relative in business has had a major impact on the terms upon which they entered British labour markets.

It should also be pointed out that after 1962 many men from the Commonwealth were also forced to rely upon a co-ethnic sponsor who would guarantee them specific jobs in Britain. This, in turn, confined many male migrants to low-paid work in ethnic businesses. But a man in this position may regard his work very differently to a woman, viewing it as entrepreneurial training (though not all men in this position realise that ambition).

At the time of writing the sexual discrimination that was built into British immigration legislation has been removed largely by reducing the rights of men, but this makes little difference to the terms upon which hundreds of thousands of women have entered Britain in the past.

A woman's place

A high proportion of Britain's ethnic minorities including men and women from India, Pakistan, Bangladesh, the Caribbean, Cyprus, and Hong Kong either originate from or have their ancestral origins in ex-British colonies (though Hong Kong remains a Crown colony), which became members of the Commonwealth. An important feature of the colonisation process was the development of an ideology alleging the innate inferiority of the dominated. Thus the plundering of whole sections of the globe could be justified in terms of imperial trusteeship for the betterment of 'backward peoples' (Fryer, 1984: 165). In 1948 the British Nationality Act conferred on citizens of what had been the British Empire (Commonwealth citizens) the right to live and work in the mother country without restriction.

But as a result of a political campaign to reduce what was called 'coloured colonial immigration', the Commonwealth Immigrants Act was passed in 1962 withdrawing the right of entry to Commonwealth citizens unless they possessed a Ministry of Labour employment voucher or unless they were a dependant of such a person. The Act appeared to rationally control labour migration without reference to race. In practice, this was not the case. In the words of Hugh Gaitskill, the then Leader of the Labour Opposition in the House: 'It is a plain anti-Commonwealth measure in theory and it is a plain anti-colour measure in practice' (Miles and Phizacklea, 1984: 42). And as William Deedes, a government minister at the time, recalled in 1968: 'The Bill's real purpose was to restrict the influx of coloured immigrants. We were reluctant to say as much openly' (ibid.: 44). The legislation was racist in intent and effect. Racism had been institutionalised from the top.

But so has sexism. Historically, British immigration law has been framed on the assumption that women are the chattels of men. The fact that over the centuries women have entered Britain on their own in search of work is not recognised in immigration law, nor the fact that those same women might want their husbands and/or children to join them.

When employment vouchers were introduced for Commonwealth citizens in 1962, women voucher holders had no automatic right to bring their husbands or children into the country while men did. The same sexual discrimination applied to holders of work permits (Women, Immigration, and Nationality Group (WING), 1985).

In the run-up to the 1979 General Election, Margaret Thatcher spoke of the legitimacy of 'people's fears' of 'being swamped' and pledged that if elected her Government would ban the entry of all foreign husbands and fiancés. A blanket ban would of course have led to the exclusion of white as well as black husbands. Opposition to the proposals reflected this concern and the rules were voted down in Parliament later in 1979. The Government hurriedly amended the proposals so as to exclude only the husbands and fiancés of women without British ancestry or put differently, mainly black women. The rules were changed again in 1983 to allow all women with British citizenship regardless of ancestry to bring in foreign husbands or fiancés, but the burden of proof to produce satisfactory evidence that the primary purpose of the marriage was not immigration was shifted from the immigration officer to the applicant. As a Commission for Racial Equality Formal Investigation into Immigration Control Procedures emphasised, it is unlikely that in the case of the genuineness of an intended marriage positive proof can be found by an applicant. The philosophy is that all applicants are bogus (Commission for Racial Equality (CRE), 1985).

Thus, minority women, according to immigration law, should stay in their own or their ancestors' country of origin and look after a husband and children. This was clearly expressed by Ivor Stanbrook, Conservative MP, in the House of Commons:

> It is part of the British way of life for the father to provide a home for the family, and it is the same in India. The husband is expected to provide the house for his wife. There is no rational argument in favour of saying that a wife in another country should be in a position to provide a home for her husband and children. It is contrary to all commonsense, human nature and the way of life of both Britain and the subcontinent.
>
> (*Hansard,* p. 1052, quoted in Barker, 1981: 23)

It is within this context of institutionalised racism and sexism that we need to consider the absorption of minority women into British labour markets and their experience of unemployment. Unfortunately, there are no recent data for Britain that cover the occupational position of all minority women. It is unfortunate because the terms (in respect of immigration legislation) upon which a number of minority groups, such as the Chinese from Hong Kong and the Greek and Turkish Cypriots, have entered Britain have been identical to what the Department of Employment refers to as 'people of ethnic minority origin' (Department of Employment, 1987: 18); the latter was referring to West Indians, Asians, and 'other non-white or mixed origins' (ibid.: 20). The Policy Studies Institute surveys refer to such groups as black, so from a number of sources we can compare the occupational position of black as compared to white women in Britain.

There have been three PSI studies carried out during the past twenty years, the last in 1982. The author, Colin Brown, concludes that Asian and Afro-Caribbean women in Britain remain largely confined to the jobs available to them or their mothers on entry to Britain. The unemployment rate in 1982 was nearly twice that of white women and the difference was even greater for the under-25 age group (according to the 1985 Labour Force Survey 44 per cent of Pakistani and Bangladeshi women were unemployed). In addition, while the 1985 Labour Force Survey indicated a continuing high level of occupational crowding of women generally, in so far as 60 per cent of black and white women are concentrated in 3 occupational groupings (clerical and related occupations, catering and cleaning jobs, and professional and related occupations in health, education, and welfare), white women were especially concentrated in clerical and related occupations (30 per cent) whereas black women were more numerous in processing and assembling occupations (Department of Employment, 1987: 25). When these occupational groupings are broken down, it is possible to begin to see the extent to which different ethnic groups are concentrated in different economic niches. Asian women are highly concentrated in manufacturing, especially textiles and clothing, and Afro-Caribbean women in professional and scientific services. The latter category accounts for 40 per cent of Afro-Caribbean women, 25 per cent of white women, 19 per cent of Indian and 7 per cent of African Asian women (Brown, 1984: 160). While these figures reflect the distribution of these ethnic groups within the National Health Service, it hides their differential occupational distribution within it. Thus, only 5 per cent of Afro-Caribbean women occupy administrative posts in the Health Service, the majority being located in nursing jobs.

I have argued elsewhere that while all minority women in the post-war period have entered a highly segregated labour market where women generally are confined to low-paid, low-status, and gender-specific employment, the work-permit system, employment vouchers, entry as dependants, and racial discrimination are all factors that compound the subordination of minority women as waged workers (Phizacklea, 1983; 1987).

In the Greater London Council's *The London Labour Plan* (1986), it is argued that the apparent similarity in the low status of black and white women:

comes from the fact that white women often find themselves trapped in low status part-time jobs. Black women are trapped in low status jobs by another mechanism – that of racial discrimination. They are much more likely to have to bring in a second wage, and to work full-time, partly because black men are also trapped in low status, low paid jobs. While full-time work lifts white women out of some of the worst low paid areas, this is much less true for black women.

(GLC, 1986: 114)

What is also clear is that while racism has prevented black women from moving to any great extent into the expanding areas of women's work, racial discrimination also results in black workers being more likely to lose their jobs than whites (Newnham, 1986).

In short, to explain the over-representation of some immigrant women (the daughters of those same women are as reluctant to enter the clothing industry as their mothers are to allow this to happen) in the sweated sector of the clothing industry, it is necessary to go beyond as Mitter says 'the patriarchal values of Asians and Cypriots', their concern about protecting the 'honour' of their women and the latter's confinement to a 'safe' working environment (Mitter, 1986: 55–7). These factors are by no means irrelevant, but it is within the broader context of structural racism and sexism that the position of clothing workers in the secondary sector of fashionwear production – some of whom work in small factories, others work in their own homes – should be considered.

Low pay and long hours

In Chapter 5 I drew attention to the price that workers have to pay to ensure the viability of the secondary-sector firms in the West Midlands clothing industry. The Low Pay Unit survey carried out in 1984 showed average earnings of £1.08 (statutory minimum £1.50). Seventy-three per cent of the workforce were working 40 hours a week or more, all were on piece rates, 64 per cent had fewer than 20 days annual holiday, and only 8 per cent were members of a union (West Midlands Low Pay Unit, 1984). If a garment was assembled in the home, the same study suggests that the worker will receive as little as 15p a garment for simple work. If, as is usually suggested, imported goods must be at least 20 per cent cheaper than domestically produced goods for retailers and manufacturers to source abroad, then we have here one very simple factor in explaining any expansion of domestic production in this sector.

In London, Bangladeshi and Cypriot interviewers were employed in March 1985 to interview a total of 17 workers outside of working hours and in their own homes. I cannot claim any kind of representativeness in the methods used in so far as the respondents were either known to the interviewers through community work, relatives, or friends. Nevertheless, the interviews that had been carried out previously on the premises of firms were, it was felt, so guarded as to be of little use. While 80 per cent of the clothing workforce is female, an effort was made to interview male machinists as well in the London industry.

What these interviews emphasise is the variability in workers' pay and hours in the London fashionwear industry, but also evidence of the way in which employers dispense with the social costs of production. For example, 7 of the 17 factory workers claimed that national insurance was not deducted from their pay and 13 said they received no holiday pay. None of the workers currently belonged to a trade union.

While it is difficult to say anything with certainty (given the numbers of workers interviewed), the workers employed for manufacturers reported more predictability about earnings and hours than any of the workers located in subcontracting firms where the flow of work was seasonal and with it their earning power.

Thus, for example, Ms M, a Cypriot, had worked as a machinist in the fashionwear industry since arriving in Britain in 1982. She currently worked for a manufacturer employing 150 workers in the factory and she estimated 50 homeworkers. She had obtained the job through a relative and without overtime she earned £80–£90 for a 40-hour week, national insurance was deducted, and she received holiday pay. With overtime she could earn £110 a week.

While three other workers interviewed were able to earn more than this, there was less predictability about basic earnings.

By comparison, Mr Y has worked as a machinist in the fashionwear industry in London since his arrival from Bangladesh in 1966. He is married with two young children. He works with only one other person for a subcontractor. His earnings varied according to the amount of hours that he worked, which was in turn seasonal. From October to December he worked 50–60 hours a week and earned around £90, in the low season his earnings went down to £65 after deductions. He said that compared to five years ago, he was working longer hours for less money. When asked whether or not he was a member of a trade union he responded, 'No, we haven't much idea about unions. . . . I remember there was a union in the clothing trades in the 1960s. I can't understand how it's been eliminated.' What was also clear was the degree of skill flexibility that he brought to his job: 'When a hard or a new style arrives there is a common understanding that we work out who can do what best.' When asked about job searches he responded, 'I have spent lots of time finding work, there isn't much work and when you find some, the money is very little compared to how hard I work. I am not getting proper money.'

But homeworkers receive even less money than those who work in factories. Mrs C was also interviewed by a Bangladeshi community worker in Tower Hamlets. Her work was again seasonal, 60 hours a week in high season (September to January), down to around 20 hours a week from January to April, and no work at all from May to August. In the high season she said she worked as much as possible because she knew that she had only 4 or 5 months in the year when she could make reasonable money. If necessary she asked friends to help her during this period. She was paid 50p for making up a skirt, £1.00 for a lady's jacket and 10p for lining. She had come from Bangladesh in 1971 and began homeworking in 1977. She added that at the time she did not even consider outdoor work because she had young children, limited knowledge of English, and cultural barriers to working outside the home. Her husband had seen an ad in the local newspaper for homeworkers. She owned her own machine, she was paid by the driver in cash, who, in season, delivered daily at 8 a.m. and collected at 6 p.m. Out of season he delivered and collected only once a week if there was work. Mrs C did not know who she worked for as she only saw the driver but she said she sewed labels into the clothes she made, including C&A labels.

In 1985 I interviewed 3 homeworkers in Birmingham to whom I was introduced by a friend. The unpredictability of the work was the major complaint of all the women. One woman was paid 35p for sewing a complete white cotton jacket that I was able to track down selling in Birmingham City Centre that week for £14.99. Another woman who did not speak English (my friend interpreted) told us that for 2 weeks the woman (middlewoman) who delivered and collected the clothes had not paid her, explaining that the work 'was not up to standard'. When she was challenged over this (the woman's daughter had received training in one of the big clothing firms in Birmingham and questioned whether her mother's product was any different to that produced indoors) she then argued that her husband had drunk the money. Mrs C pointed out that she was unwilling to carry on working in order to support her supplier's husband's drinking habit. Mrs C did not see the middlewoman again.

In 1988 Kamlesh Rai and Nasheema Sheikh of the National Homeworking Unit in Birmingham interviewed 50 homeworkers in the city. If the prices women were being paid in 1988 are compared to 1984 it is evident that homeworkers' pay had not increased – 30p for making up a skirt, 60p for a dress, and 25p for a child's dress was usual. The effective hourly rate is 80p compared to a statutory minimum of £1.98 laid down by the 1986 Wages Act.

An *Observer* newspaper 'open file' report that followed up these findings showed that supposedly 'reputable' firms supplying Marks and Spencer, Richard Shops, C&A, etc. were using homeworkers earning well under minimum rates (Harris, *Observer*, Sunday, 5 June 1988: 7).

But the hidden nature of manufacturing homework and the ambiguity of the employee relationship results in severe problems in improving the bargaining position of homeworkers, who in the eyes of the present Government 'have the same protection as other workers' (ibid.: 7).

Lifting the lid on homework

The cause of organisations that have campaigned for years to improve the position of homeworkers principally through attempting to achieve employee status for them and raise public awareness of the constraints that force many thousands of women into homeworking was not helped by the publication of Department of Employment research on homeworking from 1984 onwards. The research was explicitly designed to demonstrate the diversity of conditions and earnings in order to dispel the notion that homeworkers are women tied to the home by child-care responsibilities and forced to work for the type of low wages which we have made reference to previously. The research was based on interviews with 576 people drawn from the 90,000-strong 1981 Labour Force Survey, which was based on a random national sample. Homeworkers were widely defined covering all those who work at home and including the self-employed, freelance workers, and independent contractors. Not surprisingly, the research suggests on this basis that homeworkers are well qualified with over a quarter of the female homeworkers being graduates and their earnings traced to short working hours. Excluding all those who work from home as opposed to at home, the research estimates that there were 229,800 homeworkers (excluding child minders), only 58,750 of whom are manufacturing homeworkers (Hakim, 1987: 95). The author claimed that 'manufacturing homework is now a relative rarity' (Hakim, 1984: 10) and that ethnic minorities are under-represented in the homeworking labour force (1987). Both of these claims run counter to all the evidence I have pointed to in this book and the local homeworking campaigns.

There are, in fact, serious problems in sampling and interpretation that make such conclusions difficult to draw. The survey was based on a random national sample, whereas manufacturing homeworkers are most highly concentrated in discrete areas of the country associated with hosiery and clothing production. In addition, in London, as we have seen a traditional centre of manufacturing homeworking, the response rate was only 43 per cent and no information is given about the response rate in other inner cities. While Hakim admits that language represents one barrier for minority women working in factories and offices, there is no indication in the report that language might have been a factor in reducing response rate in the inner cities. Unless mother-tongue interviewers are used in particular localities, there is no possibility of interviewing homeworkers. For many black women, fear of attack is an additional deterrent to answering the door to a stranger. Finally, because so much homeworking is 'off the books', fear of reprisals makes many homeworkers reluctant to declare themselves.

In fact in a later report Hakim admits that 'the 1981 National Homeworking Survey does not provide any information on the proportion of all home-based workers who are ethnic minorities' (Hakim, 1987a: 45).

The extent of under-renumeration of homeworking has already been alluded to but can be further illustrated by reference to the official economic activity rates for Pakistani and Bangladeshi women in Britain, which is 17 per cent, and local studies such as Anwar's (1979) research in Rochdale where he states that most Pakistani women are homeworkers. Most homeworkers are unwilling to declare themselves either through fear of losing their jobs or coming to the notice of the authorities. Incorrectly, in most cases they believe that because they are not paying tax they are breaking the law and their suppliers use this argument to justify the low prices they pay. In fact, most of the homeworkers we encountered in the clothing industry were earning well below the tax threshold.

The experience of all the local homeworking projects is that it is only after many years of building trust between the project workers and homeworkers that the latter will feel able to talk openly about their work. The Wolverhampton Homeworkers Research Project was built on this kind of trust and drew on information gathered by Asian women from 50 Asian women homeworkers. The project set out to ascertain why women became homeworkers and to examine their employment conditions and rights. Of the 50 women 47 had children, the majority having 3 or more. Seventy-two per cent gave child care as the main reason for working at home. The majority had worked outside the home before the birth of their first child. None was currently a member of a trade union. Nearly all had had to purchase their own sewing machine at an average cost of £300 and yet their pay varied betweeen 25p and £1.00 an hour (1983). Sixty per cent of the women described themselves as being self-employed or did not understand the relationship between themselves and their employer (Wolverhampton Homeworkers' Research Project, 1984).

The advantages to employers are numerous. As long as a worker is labelled self-employed, the employer can avoid: paying the employer's national insurance contribution; deductions for PAYE; redundancy payments; unfair dismissal claims; and certain statutory and common-law duties for health and safety. In addition, the worker's speeds are of little interest to the supplier as long as she does the work in the time allotted. So, for instance, if Mr X delivers 50 skirts to Mrs Y to be made up in 4 days for collection, Mr X is not interested in whether Mrs Y can do that many in 2 days or 4 days because he is paying her by the piece. He will be worried if they are not done on time. In addition, Mr X is unlikely to be paying for the manufacturing equipment and is not paying for heating or lighting.

What are the advantages for homeworkers? In a study of new technology homeworking carried out by Ursula Huws in 1984, one responded when asked what were the main advantages of homeworking: 'Being at home all day with the kids'. When asked what were the main disadvantages of homeworking, she replied, 'Being at home all day with the kids' (Huws, 1984).

Most women believe that homeworking will resolve the problem of combining child care and the need to work for wages. Nevertheless, there is plenty of evidence to show that most homeworkers find it very difficult to work when their children are around, having to wait until they go to sleep and feeling guilt-ridden about working when they are awake. Christensen's study of white collar homeworkers in the United States showed that the majority found combining work and child care stressful and isolating (Christensen, 1985).

But because of the ambiguity of their employment position, it is very difficult for homeworkers to claim the rights and benefits of other workers. The present Government has refused to remove this ambiguity either by obliging the provider of homework to make the homeworkers' position clear or by giving all homeworkers employee status. The Government's position is that 'the providers of work would probably require the homeworker to be self-employed and this would still require the courts to establish the true position' (TUC: 1985: 16) and that legislation was not called for because homeworkers were different to other workers, that they probably prefer to be self-employed, and that there were potentially severe problems of abuse of unemployment benefit. What this reasoning reflects is a complete lack of political will to do anything about the highly exploitative relationship in which many homeworkers currently find themselves in relation to their suppliers.

My feeling is that the new conditions, that is, short runs at short notice, forced on producers by retailers, the shortage of green, trainable labour outside the inner cities, and the many advantages that accrue to employers in their use of homeworkers will result in an increased use of homeworking in the British fashionwear industry, not less.

What price fashion in the UK?

At the start of this book I stated that in a labour-intensive industry based on a globally available technology, decline was blamed on cheap imports and despite an increasingly protectionist stance against the low-wage developing countries, producers in the developed countries were advised to 'automate, relocate, or evaporate'.

I have argued that the threat of cheap imports is one that needs to be regarded with some scepticism in the fashionwear sector for a number of reasons, perhaps most importantly because the second greatest threat in terms of the value of imports comes not from a poor country but from Italy, where minimum wages are higher than in Britain. In addition imports are nothing more than the buying decisions of retailers, many of whom adopt an arm's-length approach in their buying policies.

If some of us are worried about our clothes being made in Bangkok sweatshops by 12-year-old captive girls or ethnic-minority women captive in their own homes in Birmingham and earning 80p an hour, what do we do about it? One route is bad publicity and the development of consumer resistance to buying clothes from the arm's-length retailers.

Not all retailers are sensitive to bad publicity as both the Granada 'World in Action' programme and the *Observer* 'Open file' article on homeworkers shows, but some are, having subsequently looked more carefully at the subcontracting chain from which their products emerged.

But there are other more formal mechanisms that can be developed to increase retailer accountability. The authors of *Linked by the Same Thread* have some useful suggestions. These include the need for tighter controls on the activities of multinational capital rather than imposing controls on developing countries as nations. The aim would be to ensure that retailers only source where basic workers' rights are observed, and this should include the UK. This requirement, they argue, could be built into codes of conduct governing operations of multinationals (Chisolm *et. al.,* 1986: 74).

In addition, trade policies should encourage exports from developing countries but be accompanied by the enforcement of a social clause establishing the right of workers to freely organise, enforce health and safety regulations, and outlaw the use of child labour. Trading preferences would be denied to those countries that did not comply. In the United States the Pease Reform Bill passed in 1985 states that trading preferences should be denied to countries that do not extend 'internationally recognised workers' rights to their workforces' (ibid.: 71).

How can action of this kind be enforced? At both the international and the national level, much stronger alliances have to be forged between the labour movement, women's groups, and anti-racist organisations to ensure that both companies and national governments honour such agreements (see Swasti Mitter's *Common*

Fate, Common Bond (1986a), Chapter 4 for an excellent account of international networking). Promoting policies of this kind would be a start in the wider campaign to improve pay and conditions in the clothing industry worldwide.

It has been argued forcefully in this book that the problem of low wages and poor working conditions in the clothing industry is not confined to the developing countries. The rundown of the Wages Inspectorate, an overstretched Health and Safety Executive, the refusal to ensure that all homeworkers be given employee status are a few of the indicators of the current Government's turning a blind eye to sweatshop conditions in Britain.

There are many who believe that the only future for the British clothing industry lies in a more automated production process. But let us reconsider for a moment my findings on the role of new technology in fashionwear production. First, it is an expensive route. Currently, it is predominantly those firms who are linked to the textile multinationals (though the innovator firm in Chapter 4 is not part of one of the textile giants) who have the scope for research and investment and who are thus best placed to reap the benefits of new technology. Second, such firms are also multinational in character, they do not have national loyalties and they will base their production sites in accordance with the most profitable allocation of factors including labour costs, markets, and tariffs. Third, while social clauses therefore need to be applied to the employment practices of such firms, the impact of a more automated production process does not in itself hold out the promise of better remunerated, more secure, and fulfilling jobs for the operatives concerned. What we are currently witnessing is one moment in an ongoing process of deskilling that will continue until only a handful of multiskilled workers are left. If clothing follows the same path as textiles, those workers are likely to be white men (Fevre, 1982). Research on the social relations of new technology illustrates the way in which it is effectively reproducing the traditional class, gender, and racial divisions of labour (see for instance Kaplinsky, 1984; Cockburn, 1985).

But increased automation in the primary-sector plants has knock-on effects for the secondary sector as well. We have argued that the small, predominantly ethnic-minority producers eking out a living in the subcontracting chain are currently being squeezed on two sides – such firms are on the one hand endeavouring to undercut Third World prices and on the other the speed and flexibility of goods produced with state-of-the-art equipment.

Jonathon Zeitlin has argued that the way forward for this small-firm sector is to adopt an industrial structure similar to one that has been developed in the Emilian region of Northern Italy (GLC, 1985). Faced with competition from low-wage producers in the 1970s, clothing and knitwear firms in the Emilian region moved up-market to designer-led production. Supported by the public provision of collective services and sympathetic banking and credit services, flexibility in these small firms, averaging only 4 employees, was achieved through 'the fluid network of relations between very small companies' (Totterdill, 1988: 4).

While it is argued that the structure has led to better wages for the workers involved, Totterdill questions whether the Emilian model really is as successful as it is made out to be. He cites reports of long hours being worked, the laying off of workers in slack periods, and the transfer of excess production to bordering low-wage regions in peak periods (ibid.: 5). In addition, Fergus Murray argues that the model is very much a product of its socio-political context, that is, artisan organisations rooted in the local Communist party which cannot simply be replicated elsewhere (Murray, 1987). In short, there is no reason to believe that the Emilian model represents a 'best practice' model and, even if it did, that it could be exported. In fact it would appear that the type of public-sector assistance available to firms in the Emilian area is not conditional on compliance with 'good employer' agreements. This has been a cornerstone of the policy of most local authorities towards assisting the secondary sector in the UK. In fact it was the failure in the eyes of some local politicians of any real 'policing' function by the Hackney Fashion Centre of its users that led to its demise.

Local authority interventions

A number of local authorities in Britain where clothing has traditionally been, or has become, a major employer, have chosen to intervene in their respective industries. According to Peter Totterdill (himself a senior local authority official with many years of experience in a number of locales) this has taken place for three main reasons:

1. in areas of employment decline in the industry to arrest further

job losses by supporting firms to adjust to new market conditions;

2. to attempt to make up for central government's retreat from intervention in a situation where competitor countries are still in receipt of adjustment aid;

3. to improve wages and conditions for low paid clothing workers by assisting firms to move into higher value-added production.

(Totterdill, 1989: 9)

Totterdill goes on to suggest that intervention falls into two interdependent categories. The first is *direct investment*. In the face of under-capitalisation for much of the industry, the local authority or enterprise board wholly or partly acquires the company on the condition that a programme of restructuring takes place accompanied by the adoption of good employer practices. One such venture in the West Midlands focused on a specialist fashionwear firm that produces some of the ready-to-wear range for a French couture company. Direct investment in larger firms has also been the preferred strategy of the Greater London Enterprise Board.

Totterdill argues that such intervention is less appropriate for the problems that beset the myriad small subcontractors in the industry where collective provision of services has been regarded as a more appropriate form of intervention.

Collective service provision by a local authority might include: marketing and sourcing strategies for firms; access to new technology, particularly the relatively costly CAD/CAM systems; and technical and business advice. Totterdill emphasises that wherever these services are provided there is a need for people to work closely with the trade unions to ensure that codes of conduct are implemented. He adds that experience has shown that local authorities have paid insufficient attention to the latter aspect of their intervention strategies (Totterdill, 1988: 10).

But the solution to ensuring that the benefits of up-grading firms get passed on to the workers is not simply a matter of better policing. The problems in this sector reflect the inequalities in power between multinational and small capital, between men and women, black and white. The provision of collective services for small undercapitalised firms can only bring real benefits to the workers if a whole range of other policies is enacted, many of which require international as well as national co-operation. The point can be illustrated with reference to the position of homeworkers. Ensuring that homeworkers get employee status is a first and vital step in up-grading their position as workers and the National Group on Homeworking in the UK is campaigning to achieve this. But the Group also emphasises that to ensure that the vast majority of homeworkers in the clothing industry have something approximating equal opportunities, many other structural obstacles must be overcome. These include the provision of free and adequate care of dependants, an end to racist and sexist practices including harassment and violence, the repeal of racist and sexist legislation, the adoption of a national minimum wage, and proper training and educational opportunities for homeworkers.

Conclusion

While the principal aim of this book has been to unpack the workings of the fashionwear industry, it has attempted also to illustrate at a very concrete level the intermeshing of gender, ethnic, and class relations.

I began at the top of the industry with the controlling power of the retailers and how competition in the late 1970s between retailing giants led to a changing market and marketing techniques. The trend has been away from a standardised product based on price to a highly differentiated market more heavily influenced by design. The diffusion of electronic point-of-sale equipment in shops allows retailers to analyse purchasing trends rapidly and place new orders in line with demand.

A major argument of the book is that recession, redundancy, and racial discrimination in employment have forced an increasing number of minority men into entrepreneurship and minority women to work for them. These structural factors have coincided with the changed market for clothing production with the emphasis on speed and flexibility. The coincidence has led to a flourishing small-firm sector operating in a highly precarious competitive market. Such firms can in many cases compete with developing country producers on price and also avoid the time and transportation constraints that overseas production brings with it for retailers. But profitability in such firms has been bought at the expense of poor wages, poor conditions, and often a suppression of workers' rights to organise.

With profit margins cut to the bone at the bottom of the subcontracting chain many entrepreneurs have dispensed with all or have kept only a core of factory-based workers, preferring to shift the risks of subcontracted orders onto the shoulders of a homeworking labour force.

When some homeworkers with factory-trained skills are earning as little as 50p an hour combined with the speed, convenience, and savings of producing goods very close to the market, then the attractions of using the British subcontracting chain are obvious.

Nevertheless, these conditions have led one commentator to conclude that parts of Britain now resemble 'a Third World country in our midst' (Harrison, 1983: 70). The dangers of turning a blind eye to such conditions are written large in history.

In the late nineteenth century Jewish immigrants were blamed for the sweated conditions that were widespread in the London clothing industry. The immigrations of the late 1890s intensified but did not initiate those sweated conditions. Jewish men and women confronted by racism and language barriers found work wherever they could or they made work for themselves in the highly competitive subcontracting system in clothing. A hundred years later we are confronted with the same situation except now it is Asian, Greek, and Turkish Cypriot immigrants who are blamed for the sweated conditions under which thousands work in Britain's bleak inner cities.

Efforts were made in the early nineteenth century to improve pay rates in the clothing industry by the introduction of the trade boards. The present Government is, in 1989, threatening to abolish their successors, the Wages Councils. The latter have provided the last statutory safety net against gross underpayment. Combined with the rundown of the Factory and Wages Inspectorate, one is led to question the sincerity of the Government's stated concern over pay and conditions in the industry. When many retailers' lack of accountability in their buying practices is added to this, then the picture looks even bleaker.

If this book has raised the reader's awareness of what goes on 'behind the label' and what some of the alternative courses of action for the future of the industry and its workers in Britain are, then it has achieved its principal aim.

Bibliography

Aldrich, H., Jones, T., and McEvoy, D. (1984) 'Ethnic advantage and minority business development', in R. Ward and R. Jenkins (eds) *Ethnic Communities in Business*, Cambridge: Cambridge University Press.

Alexander, S. (1983) *Women's Work in Nineteenth Century London: a study of the years 1820–50*, London: Journeyman Press.

Anthias, F. (1983) 'Sexual divisions and ethnic adaptation: the case of Greek-Cypriot women', in A. Phizacklea (ed.) *One Way Ticket*, London: Routledge.

Anwar, M. (1979) *The Myth of Return*, London: Heinemann.

Apparel International (1984) International Variations in Wage Costs per Direct Employee, February.

Barker, M. (1981) *The New Racism*, London: Junction Books.

Baxter, S. and Raw, G. (1988) 'Fast food, fettered work: Chinese women in the ethnic catering industry', in S. Westwood and P. Bhachu (eds) *Enterprising Women*, London: Routledge.

Belussi, F. (1987) 'Benetton: information technology in production and distribution: a case study of the innovative potential of traditional sectors', Science Policy Research Unit, Occasional Papers, University of Sussex.

Birnbaum, B., Evesley, J., Clouting, T., Allard, D., Hall, J., Morgan, S., Woods, K., Allan, R., and Tully, R. (1981) 'The clothing industry in Tower Hamlets: an investigation into its structure and problems', Tower Hamlets Council.

Bishton, D. (1984) 'The sweat shop report', Birmingham, All Faiths for one Race (AFFOR).

Blalock, H. (1967) *Toward a Theory of Minority Group Relations*, New York: John Wiley.

Bonacich, E. (1973) 'A theory of middleman minorities', *American Sociological Review,* 38: 538–94.

Bonacich, E. and Modell, J. (1980) *The Economic Basis of Ethnic Solidarity: Small Business in the Japanese American Community*, Los Angeles and Berkeley: University of California Press.

British Business (1984) 'Textile and clothing output falls back', pp. 598–601, 10 August.

British Business (1988) 'Textiles output highest since 1980', pp. 29–31, 26 August.

Brooks, A. (1982) *Black Business in Lambeth: Report of Survey, London,* London Borough of Lambeth, Directorate of Town Planning, Information and Research Group.

Brown, C. (1984) *Black and White Britain: The Third PSI Survey,* London: Heinemann.

Business Statistics Office (1979, 1985, 1987) *Business Monitor, PA 1003, Size Analyses of United Kingdom Businesses,* Newport, Wales: HMSO.

Business Statistics Office (various dates) *Business Monitor, PQ1006, Establishment Analysis,* Newport, Wales: HMSO.

Cable, V. (1982) 'Cheap imports and jobs: the impact of competing imports from low labour cost countries on UK employment', in P. Maunder, (ed.) *Case Studies in Economic Development,* London: Heinemann.

Cavanagh, J. (1982) 'Northern transnationals can use new MFA to sew up markets', *South,* pp. 70–1, May.

Chisolm, N., Kabeer, N., Mitter, S., and Howard, S. (1986) *Linked by the Same Thread: the Multi-Fibre Arrangement and the Labour Movement,* London: Tower Hamlets International Solidarity and Tower Hamlets Trade Union Council.

Christensen, K. (1985) *Impacts of Computer-Mediated Home Based Work on Women and their Families,* Centre for Human Environments, The Graduate School of the City University of New York.

Clark, P. and Rughani, M. (1983) 'Asian entrepreneurs in wholesaling and manufacturing in Leicester', *New Community,* 2 (1/2): 23–33.

Cockburn C. (1983) *Brothers: male dominance and technological change,* London: Pluto Press.

Cockburn, C. (1985) *The Machinery of Dominance,* London: Pluto Press.

Commission of the European Communities (1981) *Commission Communication to the Council on the Situation and Prospects of the Textile and Clothing Industries in the Community,* Com. (81) 388, Brussels.

Commission for Racial Equality (CRE) (1985) *Immigration Control Procedures: report of a formal investigation,* London: CRE.

Coyle, A. (1982) 'Sex and skill in the organisation of the clothing industry', in J. West (ed.) *Women, Work and the Labour Market,* London: Routledge.

Coyle, A. (1984) *Redundant Women,* London: The Women's Press.

Crine, S. (1979) *The Hidden Army,* London: Low Pay Unit.

Davenport, E. (1988) 'Strategic interventions in the UK clothing and textiles sector: the search for flexibility and the role of central and local state agencies', unpublished M. Phil thesis, Trent Polytechnic.

Department of Employment (1976) *The Role of Immigrants in the Labour Market,* London: Department of Employment, Unit for Manpower Studies.

Department of Employment (1987) 'Ethnic origin and economic status', *Employment Gazette,* pp. 18–29, January.

Department of Trade and Industry (1987) *Bulletin of Textile and Clothing Statistics,* annual edition, London: D.T.I.

Dex, S. (1983) 'The second generation: West Indian female school leavers', in A. Phizacklea (ed.) *One Way Ticket*, London: Routledge.

Drapers Record (1984) 11 February, p. 5.

Duffield, M. (1981) 'Racism and counter-revolution in the era of imperialism: a critique of the political economy of migration', paper presented to the Conference of Socialist Economists, Bradford, July.

Elson, D. and Pearson, R. (1981) '"Nimble fingers make cheap workers"; an analysis of women's employment in Third World export manufacturing', *Feminist Review*, 7: 87–107, Spring.

Euromonitor (1985) *The UK Clothing Report*, London: Euromonitor Publications.

Fevre, R. (1982) *The Labour Process in Bradford with Special Reference to 16–19-year-olds*, EEC/DES Transition to Work Project, Bradford College.

Frobel, F., Heinrichs, J., and Kreye, O. (1981) *The New International Division of Labour*, Cambridge: Cambridge University Press.

Fryer, P. (1984) *Staying Power*, London: Pluto Press.

Gaffikin, F. and Nickson, A. (n. d.) *Jobs Crisis and the Multi-nationals: the case of the West Midlands*, Birmingham: Trade Union Resource Centre.

GATT (1984) *Textiles and Clothing in the World Economy*, Geneva: GATT, Appendices I–IV.

Gerber, H.J. (1983) 'Visions: tomorrow's apparel production', *Bobbin*: 89-102, February.

Greater London Council, Economic Policy Group (1984) *The London Clothing Industry*, Strategy Document, No. 37, London: GLC, June.

Greater London Council, Economic Policy Group (1985) *Strategy for the London Clothing Industry: a debate*, Strategy Document, No. 39, London: GLC, May.

Greater London Council (1986) *The London Labour Plan*, London: GLC.

Hakim, C. (1984) 'Homework and outwork: national estimates from two surveys', *Employment Gazette*, 92: 7–12.

Hakim, C. (1987) 'Homeworking in Britain: key findings from the national survey of home-based workers', *Employment Gazette* 95: 92–104.

Hakim, C. (1987a) *Home-based Work in Britain: A report on the 1981 National Homeworking Survey*, Department of Employment Research Paper No. 60, London: DOE.

Hall, P. G. (1962) *The Industries of London since 1861*, London: Heinemann.

Hamilton, G. (1978) 'Pariah capitalism: a paradox of power and dependence', *Ethnic Groups*, 2: 1–15.

Harris, A. (1988) 'Hardship hides behind doors of homeworkers', *Observer*, 5 June.

Harrison, P. (1983) *Inside the Inner City: life under the cutting edge*, London: Penguin Books.

Hartmann, H. (1979) 'Capitalism, patriarchy and job segregation by sex', in Z. Eisenstein (ed.) *Capitalist Patriarchy and the Case for Socialist Feminism*, New York and London: Monthly Review Press.

Healey, M., Clark, D., and Shrivastava, V. (1988) *The Clothing Industry in*

Coventry, Industrial Location Working Paper No. 10, Coventry: Geography Department, Coventry Polytechnic.

Hoel, B. (1982) 'Contemporary clothing sweatshops, Asian female labour and collective organisation', in J. West (ed.) *Work, Women and the Labour Market*, London: Routledge.

Hoffman, K. and Rush, H. (1983) *Micro-electronics and Clothing – the impact of technical change on a global industry*, Draft Report, Science Policy Research Unit, Sussex University, Brighton.

Hollings Apparel Industry Review (1984, 1985, 1987) Manchester Polytechnic, May.

Huws, U. (1984) *The New Homeworkers: new technology and the changing location of white-collar work*, Pamphlet No. 28, London: Low Pay Unit.

International Labour Organisation (ILO) (1987) *The Impact on Employment and Income of Structural and Technological Change in the Clothing Industry*, Third Tripartite Meeting for the Clothing Industry, Report III, Geneva: ILO.

Jeffreys, J. B. (1954) *Retail Trading in Great Britain 1850–1950*, Economic and Social Studies, No. XIII, National Institute of Economic and Social Research, Cambridge: Cambridge University Press.

Jenkins, R. (1984) 'Divisions over the international division of labour', *Capital and Class*, (22): 28–58.

Jones, G. S. (1971) *Outcast London*, Oxford: Oxford University Press.

Josephides, S. (1988) 'Honour, family and work: Greek Cypriot women before and after migration', in S. Westwood and P. Bhachu (eds) *Enterprising Women*, London: Tavistock.

Kaplinsky, R. (1984) *Automation: the technology and society*, London: Longman.

Kasama (1983) Newsletter of the Philippines Support Group, Issue No. 2.

Keesing, D. R. and Wolf, M. (1980) *Textile Quotas against Developing Countries*, Thames Essay No. 23, Trade Policy Research Centre, London.

Ladbury, S. (1984) 'Choice, chance or no alternative? Turkish-Cypriots in business in London', in R. Ward and R. Jenkins (eds) *Ethnic Communities in Business*, Cambridge: Cambridge University Press.

Land, H. (1980) 'The family wage', *Femininst Review*, (6): 55–77.

Leigh, R. and North, D. (1983) *The Clothing Industry in the West Midlands*, Birmingham: West Midlands County Council Economic Development Committee.

Leigh, R., North, D., Gough, J., and Sweet-Escott, K. (1984) *Monitoring Manufacturing Employment Change in London, 1976–1981*, vol. 2, Industrial Sector Studies, Middlesex: Middlesex Polytechnic.

Light, I. (1972) *Ethnic Enterprise in America*, Berkeley and Los Angeles: University of California Press.

London School of Economics (1930) *New Survey of London Life and Labour*, vols 1 and 2, Westminster: P. S. King Ltd.

Mars, G. and Ward, R. (1984) 'Ethnic business development in Britain: opportunities and resources', in R. Ward and R. Jenkins (eds) *Ethnic Communities in Business*, Cambridge: Cambridge University Press.

Marx, K. (1977) *Capital*, vol. 1, London: Lawrence & Wishart.

Miles, R. and Phizacklea, A. (1984) *White Man's Country*, London: Pluto Press.

Mitter, S. (1986) 'Industrial restructuring and manufacturing homework: immigrant women in the clothing industry', *Capital and Class* 27: 37–80, Winter.

Mitter, S. (1986a) *Common Fate, Common Bond*, London: Pluto Press.

Morokvasic, M. (1983) 'Women in migration: beyond the reductionist outlook', in A. Phizacklea (ed.) *One Way Ticket*, London: Routledge.

Morokvasic, M., Phizacklea, A., and Rudolf, H. (1986) 'Small firms and minority groups: contradictory trends in the French, German and British clothing industries', *International Sociology*, 1: 397–420.

Murray, F. (1987) 'Flexible specialisation in the "Third Italy"', *Capital and Class*, (33): 84–95.

National Union of Tailors and Garment Workers and the Hackney Trade Union Support Group (1983) *Report on the Clothing Industry and Public Sector Investment in East London*, London: Hackney Trades Council.

NEDO, Clothing Economic Development Council (1971) *New Technology and the Clothing Industry*, London: HMSO.

NEDO (1979) *The Anatomy of Purchasing Clothing Machinery*, London: HMSO.

Newnham, A. (1986) *Employment, Unemployment and Black People*, London: Runnymede Trust.

Paglaban, E. (1978) 'Philippines: workers in the export industry', *Pacific Research*, 1 (3–4): 2–31, March–June.

Phillips, A. and Taylor, B. (1980) 'Sex and skill', *Feminist Review*, 6: 56–79.

Phizacklea, A. (1982) 'Migrant women and wage labour: the case of West Indian women in Britain', in J. West (ed.) *Work, Women and the Labour Market*, London: Routledge.

Phizacklea, A. (1983) 'Introduction', in A. Phizacklea (ed.) *One Way Ticket*, London: Routledge.

Phizacklea, A. (1984) 'A sociology of migration or race relations? A view from Britain', *Current Sociology* 32 (3): 199–218.

Phizacklea, A. (1987) 'Minority women and economic restructuring: the case of Britain and the Federal Republic of Germany', *Work, Employment and Society*, 1 (3): 309–25.

Piore, M. (1979) *Birds of Passage: migrant labour and industrial societies*, Cambridge: Cambridge University Press.

Piore, M. (1981) in S. Berger, and M.J. Piore (eds) *Dualism and Discontinuity in Industrial Societies*, Cambridge: Cambridge University Press.

Rai, K. and Sheikh, N. (1989) 'Homeworking', National Unit on Homeworking, Wolverly House, 18, Digbeth, Birmingham B6 (forthcoming).

Rainnie, A. F. (1984) 'Combined and uneven development in the clothing industry: the effects of competition on accumulation', *Capital and Class* (22): 141–56, Spring.

Roxby, B. C. (1984) 'The forgotten workers: a study of the legal problems faced by homeworkers', Leicester Outwork Campaign.

Sharpston, M. (1975) 'International subcontracting', *Oxford Economic Papers*, pp. 94–135, March.

Silbertson, Z. A. (1984) *The Multi-Fibre Arrangement and the UK Economy*, London: HMSO.

Stone, K. (1983) 'Motherhood and waged work: West Indian, Asian and white mothers compared', in A. Phizacklea (ed.) *One Way Ticket*, London: Routledge.

Tambs Lyche, H. (1982) *The London Patidor*, London: Macmillan.

Tang, S. L. (1980) 'Global reach and its limits: women workers and their responses to work in a multi-national electronics plant', mimeo, Department of Sociology, Chinese University, Hong Kong.

Totterdill, P. (1989) 'The role of local intervention: choices and agencies for change', paper presented to the Information Technology and the Clothing Industry Conference, Brighton Polytechnic, 26–7 February.

Trades Union Congress (1985) *Homeworking: a TUC statement*, London: Congress House.

van den Berghe, P. (1975) 'Asian Africans before and after independence', *Kroniek van Afrika*, 6: 197–205.

Voice of Women (1982) 'Conditions of work in the Sri Lanka FTZ according to women garment workers', *Voice of Women: Sri Lanka Journal for Women's Emancipation*, (4), July.

Waldinger, R. (1986) *Through the Eye of the Needle: immigrants and enterprise in New York's garment trades*, New York: New York University Press.

Ward, R. and Jenkins, R. (eds) (1984) *Ethnic Communities in Business*, Cambridge: Cambridge University Press.

Ward, R. and Reeves, F. (1984) 'West Indian business in Britain', in R. Ward and R. Jenkins (eds) *Ethnic Communities in Business,* Cambridge: Cambridge University Press.

Weber, M. (1958) *The Protestant Ethic and the Spirit of Capitalism*, New York: Scribner.

Weisbach, K. J. (1984) 'Humanisation problems with regard to advanced machinery technologies in the clothing industries', statement to the Tripartite Conference, Sunningdale, 7 September.

West Midlands Low Pay Unit (WMLPU) (1984) *Below the Minimum*, Birmingham: West Midlands Low Pay Unit.

Westwood, S. (1984) *All Day, Every Day*, London: Pluto Press.

Westwood, S. (1988) 'Workers and wives', in S. Westwood and P. Bachu (eds) *Enterprising Women*, London: Routledge.

Westwood, S. and Bhachu, P. (1988) *Enterprising Women: ethnicity, economy and gender relations*, London: Routledge.

Wilkins, R. (1982) 'The problems of recruitment in Hackney's clothing industry', unpublished research project, Hackney Council.

Wilson, E. (1977) *Women and the Welfare State*, London: Tavistock.

Wilson, P. and Stanworth, J. (1985) *Black Business in Brent: a study of inner London black minority enterprise*, London: Small Business Research Trust.

Wilson, P. and Stanworth, J. (1988) 'Growth strategies in small Asian and Caribbean businesses', *Employment Gazette*, pp. 8–14, January.

Wolverhampton Homeworkers' Research Project (1984) Wolverhampton Trades Council.

Women, Immigration, and Nationality Group (WING) (1985) *Worlds Apart*, London: Pluto Press.

Wray, M. (1957) *The Women's Outerwear Industry*, London: Duckworth.

Zeitlin, J. and Totterdill, P. (1988) 'Markets, technology and local intervention: the case of clothing', paper presented to the Information Technology and the Clothing Industry Conference, Brighton Polytechnic, 26–7 February.

Index